THE FIRST-TIME MANAGER:
A SURVIVAL GUIDE

THE FIRST-TIME MANAGER: A SURVIVAL GUIDE

Theodore G. Tyssen

Self-Counsel Press
(*a division of*)
International Self-Counsel Press Ltd.
Canada   U.S.A.

Printed in Canada

First edition: June, 1992; Reprinted: February, 1993

Canadian Cataloguing in Publication Data
    Tyssen, Theodore G.
    The first-time manager
    (Self-counsel business series)
    ISBN 0-88908-993-0
    1. Management I. Title. II. Series.
    HD31.T97 1992 658 C92-091170-6

Cover photo Terry Guscott, ATN Visuals, Vancouver, B.C.
Illustrations taken from 1800 Woodcuts by Thomas Bewick and His School and Children: A Pictorial Archive from 19th Century Sources, published by Dover Publications Inc., New York. Used courtesy of Dover Publications Inc.

Self-Counsel Press
(*a division of*)
International Self-Counsel Press Ltd.
Head and Editorial Office
1481 Charlotte Road
North Vancouver, British Columbia V7J 1H1

U.S. Address
1704 N. State Street
Bellingham, Washington 98225

CONTENTS

TABLES

SAMPLES

WORKSHEETS

PREFACE

This book is inspired by my experiences in management and management training over the last 30 years. It is also inspired by the need for a simplified, practical, yet comprehensive method to help new managers understand their tasks and do them well.

Like many of my contemporaries, I was thrust into management with absolutely no training or preparation for the role. In fact, I had no understanding of the concept of management other than as a "step up the ladder." Naturally, during my time as a new manager, I made the predictable mistakes — hiring the wrong people for the job, putting new employees to work "cold" with no orientation or direction, and not coaching effectively when employees needed help.

As I became aware of the large gaps in my management skills, I read books on the subject and attended as many seminars and lectures as I could. In 1974, I finally took the plunge into post-graduate work, and in 1978 earned an MBA from York University in Toronto.

My experience and education were soon put to work developing training seminars for front-line managers. "Productive Coaching," "Recruiting, Interviewing and Hiring," and "Conducting Effective Performance Appraisals" were some of the seminars I designed and presented. As I became an expert in the various management models, I began to think that there must be a way to tie all management skills into a single comprehensive model.

It was finally some of the models for training and coaching that helped me develop a comprehensive method. These models emphasize that the real problem, and the one that training and coaching must address, is often different from the apparent problem. The apparent problem is only a symptom; what is needed is a front-end analysis, or needs analysis, to get to the heart of the problem.

By applying the front-end analysis to management in general, I realized that managers need a method that does two things:

(a) simplifies managing techniques to basic steps, and

(b) orders these steps in a logical progression.

With these fundamentals in mind, I began collecting data on management skills and reducing these skills and techniques to their common denominators. While some management experts discuss as many as 25 ways of solving people problems, my research showed me that all people problems boil down to problems in 5 basic areas. All people-managing activities fit into these 5 areas.

These activities are the foundation for the 5 steps of this people-centered method. When I tested out the method in practice, I knew that I had reached my goal. I discovered that these 5 steps are not simply the most important steps in managing effectively; they are the *only* steps.

INTRODUCTION

Managing means getting things done through your employees with their full cooperation. As a manager, your success depends on what your employees do. In essence, then, managing is a people-centered activity. Effective management means solving people problems and establishing a work environment that prevents people problems from developing in the first place.

This book is designed to give new managers a practical, step-by-step method for producing the best results possible, both for themselves and for their people. It shows the influence you wield and the responsibilities you have for your people. It demonstrates efficient techniques for isolating and solving performance problems with confidence. It illustrates a pro-active method for managing people, an approach which prevents people problems before they begin.

Best of all, this approach simplifies all the management basics to five basic steps. These steps outline what you need to know and do to achieve real performance results and to maintain top quality performance over the long term.

You don't need to be new to managing to reap the benefits of this approach. Based on state-of-the-art management theory and practice, this method provides the practical update that experienced managers value to refresh their management style.

The underlying management philosophy of my approach is commonly referred to as "participative management." The focus is on building humane organizations where jobs mean more than earning money, where people are encouraged to refine their special skills, and where the phrase "increased productivity" doesn't mean layoffs and terminations. It aims at team building and at developing a highly motivated work force that shares in the mission of the organization. In short, it means commitment to people, to quality, and to customer service.

Participative management is also concerned with long-term benefits. As such, it stands in sharp contrast to the North American management mentality of the past decades, when maximizing profits over the short term was the primary goal. During that period, companies and managers emphasized quantitative methods for improving the bottom line and thus increasing earning per share by a few pennies each quarter. Many organizations are now paying the long-term costs of their short-term gains.

A people-centered management style, on the other hand, means leadership management, not manipulative management. It encourages an entrepreneurial spirit that gets all employees involved. The proven assumption at the base of this approach is that involved workers are the key to increased productivity. So when you manage with these principles, you can let the bottom line look after itself.

In the end, this five-step method creates a win-win-win situation. You, the manager, win the satisfaction of seeing your people perform at their very best. Your employees win real job satisfaction and pride in their work. And your organization wins the rewards of high productivity.

1

PEOPLE MANAGING — THE KEY TO BEING A SUCCESSFUL MANAGER

This book is based on a simple premise: all people-managing activities fit into five areas and all people problems boil down to problems in these five areas. Thus, the five steps in managing people are not just the most important steps — they are the only steps.

It is true, of course, that managing also involves planning, organizing, formulating policies and programs, collecting data, sorting data into information, reporting, attending meetings, and sharing in organizational decisions. Though these activities fall outside the realm of managing people, you can't be a really effective manager unless you're a good people manager, too.

No matter how important or how pressing your other duties as a manager become, you must deal with people issues first. If the people you supervise don't produce the expected results, you will be judged on that basis. Successful people managing is *the* critical task in creating high-performance results.

The professional practice of managing people is as challenging and complex as the practice of medicine or law. We never hear of a "one-minute brain surgeon" or a "one-minute lawyer." One minute is about how long the doctor or lawyer who tries a one-minute method will last. The quick fix and the overly simple solution have no more place in the manager's office than they do in the operating room or the courtroom. Excellence in any profession cannot be achieved overnight. You must learn the basics and then sharpen your skills in the practice of the profession. And if you want to excel, you must keep up with new thoughts and ideas on managing.

The professional practice of managing people is challenging and complex

a. JAPANESE STYLE: KAIZEN

One extremely valuable source of inspiration on managing people is the Japanese management style called *kaizen*. When applied to management, kaizen means gradual, ongoing improvement, involving everyone from top management to production workers. It emphasizes a multi-skilled, team-oriented work force as the means of boosting quality and productivity. This is people managing.

During the last decade, many North American companies have incorporated selected Japanese management practices into their overall strategy. Such innovations as quality-control circles, just-in-time manufacturing, and zero-defect standards are borrowed from the immensely successful example of what has come to be called "Japan Inc." Yet not everyone understands the concept behind these management practices, the concept of kaizen. According to Masaaki Imai, the author of *Kaizen: The Key to Japan's Competitive Success*, we suffer from a classic case of missing the forest for the trees.

One company that has understood and implemented the kaizen concept is Gen Corp. Automotive of Akron, Ohio. Here, the idea of everyone working equally as a team member has been remarkably universalized. All employees at Gen Corp's Shelbyville plant are salaried, and all receive identical parking privileges, benefits, and gain-sharing opportunities. Everyone wears identical blue pants and light blue shirts with button-down collars.

Even more important is the company's approach to selecting its people. Gen Corp. seeks employees who thrive in an environment of continued learning. According to Ray Casper, director of human resources, the aim is to develop employees who are able to do any job in the plant. Gen Corp. seeks people who are not only smart, but willing to make suggestions for improvements, help others, and do a variety of jobs. In short, people who, in a more traditional workplace might be seen as "treading on someone else's turf," are just the people Gen Corp. wants.

A Nissan plant in Tennessee uses the kaizen approach, too. In this plant, careful screening for both "can do" and "will do" factors in the hiring process has paid off in a low rate of turnover and absenteeism. In fact, the work force has become so efficient that the plant has brought in additional work in axle and engine assembly just to keep its employees occupied!

A Toyota plant in Ohio is managed along the same lines. The company is looking for people with excellent interpersonal skills; quick learners with good problem-identification and problem-solving skills; people who are able to recommend solutions, not just acknowledge that a problem exists; people who focus on the design and improvement of the job.

Forward-looking organizations know that they simply can't afford not to adopt and adapt at least some of the management practices that have made Japan the economic success story of the century.

b. THE FIVE-STEP APPROACH

To achieve this kind of success, you need a practical, understandable approach to managing your people. The five basic steps outlined below do not comprise a quick fix. Neither will they tell you all you ever need to know about managing people. What they will do, however, is get you to focus on the fundamentals of managing people. It is then up to you to learn more about each of these fundamentals. Most important, you must put the fundamentals into practice, and practice them until they become part of your management arsenal. Without practice, what you get from this book will simply be knowledge, and knowledge without practice is of little use in the workplace. Daily practice is the key to developing any skill. In mastering these steps, you master the art and science of managing people.

These steps follow a logical sequence of activities. The first two steps cover the essentials for getting a job done well — selecting the right person and directing that person in the job tasks. The last three steps cover strategies for removing obstacles which may interfere with the right person, properly directed, doing the job well.

Going through all the steps in sequence provides you with an efficient strategy for analyzing job performance problems. To pinpoint the problem, you start with step one and

4

then move through the other steps one by one. If you have no way of arriving at the real cause of the problem, expensive mistakes get made; for example, spending time, effort, and money on training when the real problem is working conditions. The five steps offer a method of isolating people problems as well as methods for solving them.

c. STEP ONE: SELECTING THE RIGHT PEOPLE

"Getting good help is shaping up as one of the biggest problems for business in the 1990s and the solutions will remake the workplace. How can you compete if you can't find the right workers?" reads an article in *Report on Business Magazine*, from June, 1990.

As the article suggests, the lean and mean business environment of the 1990s won't tolerate a haphazard approach to hiring and promoting. Today's organizations know that selecting the right people for the right task, and thereby building an efficient, highly motivated work force, is critical to their success. And they know that all the training, motivating, and directing in the world will not compensate for hiring the wrong person. Once the wrong person is hired for a job — like a round peg forced into a square hole — the productivity on this job will be forever deficient. It is easy to see, then, that selecting the right people is the first step in managing people.

d. STEP TWO: PROVIDING JOB ORIENTATION AND ONGOING DIRECTION

Once you have selected the right person for the job, you must tell him or her what the job is all about. Even when the person you have selected has done a similar job before, you need to tell him or her exactly what is expected on this particular job.

When the employee is new to the organization, orientation to the specific tasks of the job is not enough. Employees need to understand the aims of the whole organization to see how their jobs fit in the total scheme of things.

A new and inexperienced employee will perform a task by choosing what he or she sees as the best method. Naturally, the selection of alternatives is limited by the employee's experience, and his or her choice may be inappropriate for your organization. Your organization has developed policies, programs, and work methods that are based on its unique experiences. These approaches and their rationales must be communicated to new employees before these people can be expected to do their jobs. It makes sense, therefore, that once you have selected the right people, the next step is to orient them and to provide continuous direction about the jobs for which they were selected.

e. STEP THREE: DESIGNING THE WORK ENVIRONMENT

Your managing task is not over when you hire the right person, orient him or her thoroughly, and provide ongoing direction. There are several other factors that influence how well employees perform. Controlling these factors is an essential part of your management task.

Conditions in the workplace certainly affect productivity. Perhaps the workspace prevents employees from performing at their best. Perhaps it is too enclosed or too exposed, too noisy or too quiet. A workspace that makes people want to work is not a luxury or a status symbol — it is a necessity. Either you pay for it when you create the space, or you pay for it in lost productivity.

The work environment is more than just where people work. The lack of proper tools or materials, equipment breakdown, or other people who interfere with job performance — these problems also contribute to poor performance. Identifying and correcting them is an essential part of your people-managing job.

f. STEP FOUR: APPLYING TRAINING AND SKILLS DEVELOPMENT

Even willing employees working under good working conditions are hampered if they lack appropriate skills and development. So pinpointing skill deficiencies and applying the right training and development is essential to managing people.

Remember, however, that of the billions of dollars spent on training and development in North America today, much is wasted. Training cannot solve the problems created by the wrong person in the job or deficiencies in the work environment. Training can remedy only deficiencies in job skills. As a manager, then, your task is to apply training as a solution only when specific skill deficiencies have been clearly identified as the problem.

g. STEP FIVE: MOTIVATING YOUR PEOPLE

Motivation is a critical factor in fostering people's willingness to work. A motivating environment produces employees who do better or more work, and want to contribute and learn more. Effective people managers are those who inspire their people to work to their full potential in every aspect of their jobs.

To do their best, today's better-educated and informed employees need to know more than simply their job functions. They need to know why they are doing what they do. They need the freedom to change job procedures when they discover a better way of doing a task. They need to have some say in decision making that concerns them. In short, they need to feel pride in their contribution.

Most of all, they need managers who recognize and work to fulfill these needs. These are the managers who will provide the high-quality motivation that gets measurable, high-quality results.

Do Worksheet #1 now and discover how many people-managing strategies you currently use. When you have finished this book and have been using your people-managing skills for sometime, take this test again. You will see the difference.

WORKSHEET #1
ANALYZING YOUR
PEOPLE-MANAGING STRATEGIES

Picture your current position and the employees who report to you. Then, answer the following questions truthfully.

1. Do you deal with "people issues" before you concern yourself with the "doing" part of the job?

Always ❏   Usually ❏   Seldom ❏

2. Do you practice the fundamentals of managing people?

Always ❏   Usually ❏   Seldom ❏

3. Do you use a logically-ordered model of people-managing principles to help you with the complex art and science of managing people?

Always ❏   Usually ❏   Seldom ❏

4. Do you think that your people are working at peak performance?

Always ❏   Usually ❏   Seldom ❏

5. Do you think that your people believe that you are the very best you can be?

Always ❏   Usually ❏   Seldom ❏

2
STEP ONE:
SELECTING THE RIGHT PEOPLE

a. THE SHIFT FROM EMPLOYEE TO MANAGER

I recall vividly how my own management career got started over 30 years ago. I was a sales rep in a small branch office of a company which supplied power transmission products. When the manager of my branch was transferred to the head office, I was promoted to replace him. As an ambitious young man, I was naturally proud of this, my second promotion. Two years before, I had moved up from inside clerk to sales rep.

Looking back now, with a view seasoned by a humility that young man lacked, I can see clearly that the company gave very little thought to my suitability for the job. No one evaluated my competency. No one suggested any preparation for my new responsibilities. I wasn't even given a job description. This approach to selecting people is called "warm body" placement. As the nearest warm body, I had been moved in to fill a gap.

To be honest, it didn't occur to me to request a job description, since I didn't give any more thought to the move than my superiors did. I was satisfied simply to rise another step on the organizational ladder.

Neither that ambitious young man nor his company recognized the significance of that promotion — the change from performing assigned tasks to managing people. The shift from worker to manager is the most important step — and the biggest change — in anyone's career. But I just rolled on, unaware of the milestone. What's worse, my company seemed unaware that as a manager, my successes and failures could make a difference to the entire organization.

Fortunately for both me and the company, most organizations took a similar approach in those post-war years. The business environment seemed to tolerate the incompetency of companies and managers, assuming that the trial-and-error method of selecting people would somehow work out to everyone's benefit in the end.

The lean and mean business environment of the nineties, however, just won't support such an approach to hiring and promotion. Today's organizations know that selecting the right people for the right tasks and building an efficient, highly motivated work force is critical to their success. And as a manager, selecting the right people is an essential part of your job.

The selection method outlined in this chapter simplifies the task, spelling out the hiring essentials you need to do the job with confidence.

b. GETTING READY TO HIRE

A simple example illustrates the importance of hiring the right person for the job. Assume that you're the coach of a professional basketball team. The owner of the club has hired a new player — his out-of-work nephew who is 5'4" tall. How would you assess your chances of making him into a competent pro basketball player — even if the fellow is an outstanding athlete? You know from the start that the very best job orientation, combined with the finest motivating and training techniques in the world, just won't help this player against the competition on the court. For everyone's sake, the owner should find his nephew another job — one for which he is suited.

Although suitability for many jobs is measured in knowledge and skills rather than physique, the basketball player example illustrates an essential in any hiring situation: the need to match the person with the requirements of the job.

Even the most skilled and successful people in the job-training field tell us that no amount of specialized training can correct all the problems caused by selecting an unsuitable person for the job. Doug Bray was a trainer at AT&T for over 30 years. He implemented the Management Progress Study and introduced ground-breaking behavior modelling techniques in supervisory training. He summarized his experience succinctly in an interview published in the February, 1988 edition of *Training,* a well-known human resources magazine. According to Bray, "First you have to select the right people; then you train them."

Doug Bray knows from long experience that the chances of hiring and placing the wrong person are very real — especially with the "warm body" method of selection. And these mistakes are always very difficult, if not impossible, to correct later, no matter how strong the training effort.

On the plus side, however, the benefits of selecting the right person are almost immeasurable. Lower turnover, lower costs for training and development, greater productivity, and more profits are among the benefits reaped by the organization. Furthermore, the employee and the manager benefit too, as both share the credit and satisfaction of doing their jobs well.

Matching the right person with the job is essential — and the method for doing it is quite simple, since it really boils down to two steps —

(a) define the job, then

(b) measure the candidates according to the competencies required to do the job effectively.

Remember that all jobs require two kinds of competencies: "can do" and "will do." "Can do" means skills and knowledge — the capabilities to do the job. "Will do" means motivators and attitudes — the willingness to do the job well.

Measure the candidates according to the competencies required

c. DEFINING THE JOB REQUIREMENTS

In hiring, as in any search process, you need to know what you're looking for before you can find what you want. The more precise your idea of the job, the more focused your screening of candidates. When you understand the competencies the job requires, you will know just how to screen applicants and just what questions to ask candidates in the interviews.

13

In gathering precise information about job requirements, you will find the following sources useful:

(a) The job description

(b) Performance appraisals of people who have done the job

(c) The direct superior (perhaps you)

(d) People who currently do or have done the same job or a similar job

(e) People who have contact with the employee filling the position — employees in other departments, clients, customers, and outside vendors

The written job description is the obvious place to start in your research. However, these descriptions often lack the detail you require to outline the full range of competencies needed for the job. Performance appraisals describing how people have done the job in the past can help fill in the specifics. Look for the factors that made people successful in the job, as well as the characteristics that interfered with their effective performance. These are important clues about what to look for and what to avoid in selecting the next person.

People as well as documents can provide very useful information about the job. Ask others about the job requirements, and consider the goals and objectives of the organization for the next year, as well as your department's goals. What specific projects will the employee in that job be dealing with in order to meet those goals?

If you draw on the experiences of other people who know what the job entails, as well as on your own experience, you'll have valuable information. Add to this any documentation about the job and you'll be able to arrive at a complete and well-defined picture of the qualities that make for success in that position.

d. DEFINING "CAN DO" FACTORS

"Can do" factors — the qualities that ensure that a person is capable of doing the job — fall into two categories: skills and knowledge. Skills are specific, measurable abilities that can be taught and, with few exceptions, can be learned by everyone. Knowledge, on the other hand, refers to a person's ability to select appropriate skills and to use them in combination with one another. Most jobs demand both skills and knowledge.

Using a clerk/typist's job as an example, let's examine the significant differences between skills and knowledge.

Skills:

- typing at 50-60 wpm
- operating a switchboard
- operating a word processor
- spelling with accuracy

Knowledge:

- screening telephone calls
- arranging meetings
- opening and routing mail
- proofreading

The activities listed under "skills" are specific and measurable abilities, while the activities listed under "knowledge" require several skills in combination, as well as some judgment as to how and when to use them.

For example, to screen phone calls tactfully and effectively, the clerk/typist must be a good communicator with strong interpersonal skills. Informed judgment is necessary for deciding whether the call is important or not. Arranging meetings also requires strong communication and interpersonal skills, along with an understanding of meeting protocol: agendas, schedules, and minutes. To route mail properly, the employee needs to read well, to understand the structure and hierarchy of the organization, and to know the division of job functions within the organization. Proofreading requires not only reading and spelling skills, but also composition skills and grammar as well as familiarity with the organization's communication style.

As you can see from this example, the mastery of specific and measurable skills doesn't necessarily guarantee the knowledge required for performing these more sophisticated tasks effectively. Our clerk/typist could be very capable of dealing with a multi-line telephone system, but incapable of screening calls. That's why it's important to consider both knowledge and skills when you define the requirements for a job.

Finally, in determining the "can do" factors, you need to consider how much creativity the job requires. Is the employee expected to develop new ideas, strategies, tactics, policies, and procedures, or to translate abstract ideas and general concepts into practical formats and procedures? If so, then the "can do" factors for the job may also include special training, education, experience, and intellectual skills.

e. DEFINING "WILL DO" FACTORS

You will notice that whenever you ask supervisors about what qualities they need in their people, they will always add something like this after they list a few technical skills: We need somebody who is motivated and ambitious. Or: We need someone who is flexible. Or: I need someone I can rely on to get the job done on time.

All of these qualities fall under the "will do" category. And none of them is as cut and dried — or as easy to assess — as the "can do" factors. It's easy to determine if a job candidate types 60 wpm, but it's not so easy to establish whether he or she likes learning new things or works efficiently under the pressure of tight deadlines.

Some understanding of human behavior certainly helps in defining the "will do" factors of any job. Abraham Maslow, a psychologist who studied human behavior in the 1950s, developed a system for categorizing people into basic types. Since his categories are based on people's motivating needs and their related behavior, Maslow's system is particularly valuable for defining "will do" factors — and selecting the person with the appropriate "will do's" for the job.

Maslow found that although each person combines needs and behaviors in a unique blend, most people fit into one of the basic types according to their dominant need, the need that motivates much of their behavior. As the following descriptions in Table #1 show, these categories can be very useful in helping managers match the right people to the right job.

As you can probably see from reading these descriptions based on Maslow's theory, the workplace offers jobs well suited to people fitting each of the four types. No personality type is "better" than another. However, people of one type may be better suited to the "will do's" of a particular job than people of another type.

For example, if the clerk/typist position described earlier requires someone who is steady, patient, persistent, and loyal, then a Type 1 person would be comfortable and effective in the job. However, if the job also requires a person capable of supervising others, a Type 4 person might be a better choice.

If you first determine which *type* of person would best carry out the tasks a job requires, you will be in a strong position to select the right individual. Deciding which type of behavior predominates in any person usually doesn't take very long. Job interviews give you sufficient opportunity to

TABLE #1
BASIC BEHAVIORAL TYPES

TYPE	DOMINANT NEED	BEHAVIOR	MOTIVATING NEEDS	ATTITUDES	STRENGTHS
1	Security	Speaks cautiously. Doesn't commit self. Says little. Procrastinates. Relies on past experience. Dislikes change and prefers routine. Shrinks back. Pessimistic. Somewhat negative.	Status quo Low risk Tradition Job security Stability Proven value Proven outcome	Loyal Steady Restful Impersonal	Ability to stay at one work station Rhythm and coordination in repetitive work Ability to cope with lack of upward mobility Persistence with boring work Steadiness in following established work patterns
2	Social	Outgoing. Talkative. Unhurried. Has a good word for everyone. Eager to please. Quick to agree. Roams from topic to topic. Has trouble making up mind.Quick to compromise. Dodges touchy subjects.	Acceptance Recognition Popularity Approval Doing good	Gregarious Articulate Impulsive Cheerful Emotional	Ability to initiate contact with strangers Ability to organize various types of people Ability to remedy human grievances Ability to create a pleasant environment Poise and mastery of language
3	Esteem	Likes status symbols. Dislikes losing. Quick to jump to conclusions. Seeks control. Tends to impatience. Uses force to overcome obstacles. More concerned with short term than long term.	Status Importance Prestige Power	Domineering Egocentric Aggressive Direct Confident	Ability to make unpopular decisions Ability to act decisively Ability to overcome obstacles Ability to achieve goals — departmental, functional, personal. Confidently competitive.
4	Independence and self-realization	Makes the best of personal resources. Inquiring. Curious. Wants to learn. Takes intelligent risks. Likes change. Enjoys challenge. Doesn't mind being proven wrong. Openly shares information. Willing to experimen.	Autonomy Privacy Control Responsibility Thorough Tactful	Determined Accurate Systematic Analytical	Ingenuity in creating new methods and procedures. Vision to plan ahead on a large scale. Cooperative yet assertive. Readiness to defend own ideas while listening to others. Reserves the right to challenge the experts. Finishes what has been started.

observe the behavior of the applicants and to narrow the field to those who best fit the behavioral type you are seeking.

Over the years, researchers and human resources experts have built on Maslow's system, adding labels and descriptions to his basic model. These alternate descriptions, described in Table #2, may give you further insight into the four basic types and help you clearly define the "will do" factors of any job you are looking to fill.

f. DESIGNING A SELECTION SHEET

Once you have determined the specific "can do" and "will do" factors for the job, you will need a selection sheet for scoring each candidate according to the criteria you have chosen. Sample #1 offers an example of a selection sheet designed to assess candidates for their "can do" and "will do" potential. The job in this sample is for a clerk/typist, but the sheet could be easily adapted for any position. Just remember that a specific list of "can do's" and "will do's" is your most important tool in selecting the right person for the job.

Notice that the sheet in Sample #1 contains the category, "Other factors." This category is for listing job requirements that don't readily fit under "can do" or "will do" and aren't subject to numerical evaluation: bondability, weekend work, extensive travel, security clearance, a driver's license, and so on.

As this sample shows, the criteria under "Other factors" may be important as "knock-out" factors — qualifications that are essential for the job. Without one or some of them, a candidate might be automatically disqualified. For example, if you are selecting a truck driver, you will certainly look for candidates with a valid driver's license.

In developing your own selection sheet, you may decide to assign different values to the selection criteria listed in the left column. For example, you may consider the "will do" factors twice as important as the "can do" factors for a particular

TABLE #2
BASIC BEHAVIORAL TYPES
APPLIED TO THE WORKPLACE

SYSTEM A (MASLOW) TYPE	DOMINANT NEED	SYSTEM B	SYSTEM C
1	Security	EXPERTS Diligent workers. Find satisfaction from mastering challenges. Concerned with performing rather than helping others.	COMPREHENDERS "Show me" attitude. Suspicion of power until can see predictable pattern. Disciplined use of time.
2	Social	HELPERS Good at smoothing conflicts. Value acceptance based on common humanity rather than performance.	SUPPORTERS High priority on friendships, relationships, cooperative behavior.
3	Esteem	DEFENDERS Rewards in getting results and triumphing over enemies. Concerned with power. Want to be treated with dignity.	DIRECTORS Want it done now, their way. Know what they want, where they're going, how to get there quickly.
4	Independence and self-realization	SELF-DEVELOPERS Excited by learning. Seek a balanced life. Change jobs easily. Drawn to the professions or to self-employment.	CATALYSTS Easily change course, impatient to seek most exciting vision for themselves and others. May forget to address specifics.

SAMPLE #1
SELECTION SHEET

Position ___Clerk/Typist___ Date_____

Candidate_____ Selector_____

POSITION CRITERIA	RATING OF CANDIDATES					
Rating	Superior (+5)	Good (+3)	Adequate (Nil)	Deficient (-3)	Lacking (-5)	Score
Can Do (Skills and knowledge)						
Education						
Work history						
Typing — 50 wpm						
WP experience						
Spelling						
Social skills						
Communication skills						
Telephone skills						
Mail routing						
Proofreading						
Meetings						
Will Do (Appropriate behavior)						
Loyalty						
Steadiness						
Stick-to-itiveness						
Repetition						
Pressure						
Mobility						
Other factors						
Overtime						
Transportation						
Totals						

job. If you list twice as many "will do" as "can do" factors, you will automatically double the weight of the "will do's."

g. INSURING AGAINST HIRING MISTAKES

Sometimes even experienced managers make mistakes and hire the wrong person for the job. To protect against this possibility, you should always specify a probationary period for new employees. It makes sense to adjust the length of probation to the complexity of the job, with a minimum of three months for a simple position and a maximum of one year for a highly complicated job.

A performance appraisal scheduled toward the end of the probationary period offers the appropriate occasion for advising an employee of your final decision and explaining the reasons for it. If you decide to terminate the employment, make it clear that you aren't labelling the employee as "inferior." Simply explain why he or she is not well suited for this particular job and would be more comfortable in another position.

At the end of the probationary period, if you are unsure whether the employee suits the job, simply extend the probation. That way, you can assure the right decision for you, for the employee, and for the organization.

h. SUMMARY

Selecting the right people for the job is your most important activity as a manager, since no department or organization can run smoothly without the right people. Your chances of finding them increase considerably when you go through the following steps:

(a) Use resources to research the requirements for any position, including —

    (i) the job description,

    (ii) performance appraisals of people who have done the job,

(iii) the direct superior (perhaps you) for the position,

(iv) people who currently do or have done the same job or a similar job, and

(v) people who have contact with the employee filling the position, such as employees in other departments, clients, and outside vendors.

(b) Define the requirements for the job, listing all the "can do" and "will do" factors, as well as any other factors necessary for performing the job tasks.

(c) Examine Maslow's four types to determine which personality type best fits the "will do" factors for the job.

(d) Using a selection worksheet that details the job requirements, assess candidates on their match with the "can do," "will do," and other factors.

(e) Specify a probationary period appropriate to the job and schedule a performance appraisal toward the end of that period.

Use Worksheet #2 to analyze a position that you currently supervise. Using this information, you are now well prepared to create a selection sheet.

For more on choosing the right people for the job, see *A Small Business Guide to Employee Selection*, another title in the Self-Counsel Series.

WORKSHEET #2
ANALYZING A POSITION

Consider one of the positions currently reporting to you. Define the selection factors for this position in the following three categories:

1. CAN DO factors required for the position

_____

_____

_____

_____

2. WILL DO factors required for the position

_____

_____

_____

_____

3. OTHER factors required for the position

_____

_____

_____

_____

4. What sources did you use to arrive at these factors?

_____

_____

_____

_____

3

STEP TWO:
PROVIDING JOB ORIENTATION
AND ONGOING DIRECTION

Howard Hughes decided at one point in his tumultuous career that he wanted to develop the world's first steam-powered car. After hiring a team of automobile design experts, he gave them these instructions: "Do whatever is necessary to develop a steam car."

After several years' work, the engineers eagerly invited Hughes to come and see the finished prototype. The members of the team were proud of their accomplishment, since they had cleverly solved the major problem posed by the project: recycling the steam so that the car didn't have to stop for water every few miles. A honeycomb of pipes throughout the entire chassis, doors and all, condensed the steam back into reusable water.

Hughes walked around the prototype car, opening the doors and kicking the tires. He then turned to the engineers and asked, "What would happen to the driver and passengers in an accident?" After an embarrassed silence, the engineers admitted that the driver and passengers would be endangered in an accident. In fact, a collision could rupture the steam pipes and boil them alive.

Horrified by the prospect, Hughes ordered that the prototype steam car be destroyed. And that was the end of his innovative invention.

What had gone wrong? The mistake was a simple management oversight, but one that wasted a lot of money as well as several years of effort. Hughes had failed to explain to the engineers at the beginning of the project exactly what he wanted — a *safe* steam-powered car. Because he missed this all-important management step, his engineers created a lobster-mobile instead.

To be an effective manager, you have to take positive steps to prevent such disasters as the lobster-mobile. Don't set vague goals and then sit by, just waiting to blame the employees for the often-predictable failure. Take responsibility, from first to last, for providing the orientation and direction employees need to understand the project and to perform their tasks well. Employees deserve to know precisely what the project is intended to achieve as well as what is expected of each of them.

In this chapter, you'll learn the basic principles for giving your employees the orientation and direction they need to do the job well. You'll find that the rewards are not only a productive work force, but employees who share your satisfaction with their work.

a. UNDERSTANDING HOW PEOPLE WORK

Dr. George A. Kelly, a professor of psychology, did some research that provides a basis for understanding what effective job orientation involves. He started at the very core of things by studying why people do what they do.

His first observation was that people are active organisms, always in motion, always taking action. And because they are always active, people are constantly choosing their actions from the alternatives available to them. His second observation was that, out of all the choices they are aware of at the moment, people always select the one that they believe to be the best.

In short, Dr. Kelly discovered that, contrary to popular opinion, people do not go through life deliberately doing illogical things. They do what they believe to be right and logical. They select the best alternative among the choices they are aware of at any particular moment.

For example, a new and inexperienced employee will perform a task by choosing what he or she sees as the best method. Naturally, the selection of alternatives is limited to those within the employee's experience, and his or her choice may seem quite illogical to someone who sees more alternatives or knows that the choice selected simply will not work.

In some jobs, there is only one workable alternative and the person doing that job must know this. For example, a person who attaches brakes to cars on an assembly line must do the job the one right way. Any other way might endanger the lives of drivers and passengers. In other jobs, however, especially those that involve dealing with people, a number of alternatives might work. People who have these kinds of jobs must be aware of a large number of alternatives and be capable of selecting the appropriate one for each situation.

When we say that someone does not have enough experience, we are actually saying that he or she is not aware of all the alternatives, or not aware that only one alternative will work in a particular situation. Inexperience is a problem faced by every employee in a new job, no matter how "smart" the employee.

b. ORIENTING EMPLOYEES TO THE JOB

As a manager responsible for inexperienced employees, you can also choose between two alternatives in dealing with job orientation. You can take the bad, old-fashioned approach, which leaves the employee to muddle through, learning the alternatives by trial and error over weeks, months, even years. This approach assumes that employees will "get it right" by working harder and longer.

The best alternative, however, is to take responsibility for assuring that the employee is given all the information necessary to make the right choices from the start. Once aware of all the alternatives, the employee can work smarter instead of harder.

Of course, a brief orientation is all that's required for some jobs, while learning other jobs may take years. Whatever the timeline, all job orientations must include periodic follow-ups or appraisals to ensure that the employee fully understands and applies the information on the job. And if for some reason the job changes, you must see that the orientation also changes to fit the new situation.

In one sense, job orientation never ends. As a manager, you are always trying to find ways to help your people improve their performance. And when new challenges come along, it's your responsibility to help them meet the new goals and expectations.

One way to provide ongoing direction is through an annual performance plan or work plan for each employee.

c. THE PERFORMANCE PLAN

1. What is a performance plan?

A performance plan details two main points:

    (a) The results expected of the employee

    (b) The ways by which the employee is to achieve them

The "results" section is primarily quantitative, for example, how much, by when; the "ways" section is more qualitative, for example, what behavior is expected to achieve the results. The quantitative section specifies the what, when, where, and why:

    (a) What: Develop a microfiche system for all itemized bills to eliminate preparation, matching, in-filing, out-filing and micro-filming of 4,000 records per month.

    (b) When: To be operational by June 30

    (c) Where: At headquarters

(d) Why: Estimated savings of $20,000 per year

The qualitative section outlines how the objectives are to be accomplished:

(a) Prepare procedures and flow charts for the new system.

(b) Train clerks to phase out the old system and put the new system into effect.

(c) Discontinue preparation of old folders.

(d) Maintain file of registration forms and deliver to all supervisors.

(e) Train file room staff.

(f) Check bills for accuracy and completeness.

(g) Maintain file of bills.

(h) Prepare new folders.

The qualitative or "how-to" section also includes target dates for completing each task.

For more detail, see the performance plans in Samples #2 and #3. These examples are based on actual performance plans currently in use in an organization.

2. Why use a performance plan?

Even if you have never used a performance plan, you can certainly imagine its benefits for both managers and employees. Employees know exactly what is expected of them for that period (usually, one year), and so they tend to work with confidence and efficiency. And managers find performance plans invaluable for measuring progress at interim follow-up meetings and as guides for performance appraisals.

In fact, performance plans designed to fit each job are a wonderful substitute for standardized performance appraisal forms. The "off-the-shelf" performance appraisal

**The Baker Museum
Performance Plan**

Date: January 15, 1992

Name: Cassandra Herald

Position: Manager — Administration/Finance

Supervisor: Mary Chancellor

Period: Fiscal 1991

Starting Date: February 1, 1991

Completion
Date: January 31, 1991

Follow-up
Meetings: April 13, 1991
                   June 15, 1991
                   September 14, 1991

Appraisal Date: January 11, 1992

Theme: Service and Support for
                   the Enterprise Performance Plan

Cassandra Herald,
Manager — Administration/Finance
For fiscal year 1991
Theme: Service & Support for the Enterprise
(Consolidating the Team)

a.Quantitative Objectives

1. (10 points)To assure the timely production of regular financial statements within 10 working days of month end and year-end statement within 30 days of year end.

2. (10 points)With the Director, to implement the planned changes to Museum entranceway and counting system by February 28, 1991.

3. (10 points)With the Director, to effect the completion of physical changes to Museum office areas by March 30, 1991.

4. (5 points)To ensure that all approved department positions are filled no later than June 15, 1991.

5. (10 points)To achieve departmental budget objectives:
      —minimum objective: approved budget
      —stretch objective: approved budget less 5%

6. (10 points)To gather information, format and produce a Museum Personnel Manual in keeping with Baker Co. policy by September 30, 1990.

7. (10 points)With the Manager of Retail Operations, to investigate and implement such control systems as are necessary to record, track and analyze the following retail concerns:
      —food costs
      —bar costs
      —labor costs
      —food inventory
      —beverage inventory
      —gift shop inventory

8. (10 points)To develop and implement performance plans for the supervisors in Finance/Administration — namely, the Clerical Supervisor, the Accounting Supervisor, the Building Supervisor and the Computer Technician.

9. (10 points)To hold at least three interim follow-up meetings and one Performance Appraisal Meeting with each department supervisor (more often for those new to their position and/or not at job rate) during fiscal 1991.

10. (5 points)With the Director, to initiate in a timely fashion during fiscal 1991 all capital and maintenance projects allowed for in the budget.

11. (5 points)By November 30, 1991, to develop recommendations concerning long-term computer applications at The Baker Museum.

12. (5 Points)To manage budget preparations for fiscal 1992 in keeping with the established form and time schedule.

b.Qualitative Objectives

1. To provide opportunity for department training to increase skill levels and productivity.

2. To foster interdepartmental training opportunities, particularly as they apply to computer applications.

3. To develop and carry out the role of Manager of Administration/Finance by delegating, coaching, counselling, teaching, motivating and developing the Clerical Supervisor, Accounting Supervisor, Building Supervisor, and Computer Specialist. The goal is to give day-to-day responsibility and accountability to these positions.

4. To foster the shared decision-making process by encouraging the four supervisors to constantly consult with the Manager of Administration/Finance, actively seek counsel, negotiate approvals, report results, communicate problems and opportunities.

5. To foster the shared decision-making process by actively encouraging the four supervisors to develop relationships with their subordinates as described in 4.

6. By self-directed learning, to keep up to date on issues of finance and accounting, personnel, and management, and thus give timely and topical advice to the Executive Director and Director on these matters.

7. With the Director, to undertake orientation to the building and the building systems, facilitating a smooth transfer of responsibilities by January 31, 1992.

8. Throughout 1991, to continue efforts and training in improving written and verbal communication.

9. To develop an understanding of the requirements of becoming a key person on the Museum's Management Team, and to communicate this role as a team player to the Administration/Finance Team.

10. To communicate with the Board of Directors, Directors, Treasurer and Secretary of the Baker Museum Foundation on matters pertaining to Finance and Personnel Administration in a manner that reflects well on the Museum Organization.

PERFORMANCE PLAN

DATE:	February 9, 1992
NAME OF EMPLOYEE:	William Jackson
POSITION:	Clerical Services Supervisor
YEAR OF PERFORMANCE PLAN:	Fiscal 1992
STARTING DATE:	February 1, 1992
COMPLETION DATE:	January 31, 1992
FOLLOW-UP MEETINGS:	June 11, 1992
December 10, 1992
APPRAISAL MEETINGS:	April 30, 1992
September 10, 1992
THEME:	Service and Support for the Enterprise

William Laureate, Clerical Services Supervisor
Fiscal 1992

a. Quantitative Objectives

1. To produce or have produced by someone else all regular business correspondence by the end of the next business day.

2. To produce or have produced all other correspondence or assignments by the negotiated completion date.

3. To ensure that deadlines for payroll input are met by either entering the data or assigning the data entry to an approved person.

4. To complete the payroll journal and related reports by five working days after the last day of the payroll period.

5. To complete weekly payroll reports by the end of every Tuesday.

6. In coordination with Museum Operations, to ensure that the reception desk is staffed for weekends, early evenings and other requested times, and that the schedule is posted at least a week in advance.

7. To ensure that all approved clerical services positions are filled no later than March 15, 1990.

8. With the Office Manager, to research the mail machine market in order to advise on alternatives at the expiry of our current machine contract in April, 1992.

9. By April 30, 1992, to produce and implement a guidelines and standards manual for the Museum's external and internal communications.

10. With the Microcomputer Specialist, to develop and implement by May 31, 1992 an in-house training seminar and reference manual for the Museum's Wordperfect users.

11. To complete the Record of Employment for normally terminated employees by July 31, 1992.

12. To assist the Office Manager in preparing forecasts for the Clerical Services budget for fiscal 1993 by August 31, 1992.

13. To achieve the Clerical Services budget objectives:

—minimum objective: approved budget

—stretch objective: approved budget less 5%

14. To execute performance plans for the Clerk/Typist and Receptionist.

15. To hold at least three interim follow-up meetings and one performance appraisal meeting with each subordinate (or more often for those new to their position and/or not at job rate) during fiscal 1992.

b. Qualitative Objectives

1. To maintain the standards of internal and external communication according to the Museum's established guidelines.

2. To provide opportunity for staff training to increase skill levels and productivity, especially with respect to telephone and greeting skills.

3. To maintain the highest quality image and presentation among reception staff by ensuring their familiarity with established procedures and guidelines.

4. To develop and carry out the role of Supervisor of Clerical Services by delegating, coaching, counselling, teaching, motivating and leading by example, and to develop the day-to-day responsibility and accountability of those in the positions of Clerk/Typist and Receptionist.

5. To foster the shared decision-making process by encouraging the Clerical Services staff to constantly consult with the Supervisor of Clerical Services, actively seek counsel, negotiate approvals, report results, communicate problems and opportunities.

6. To foster the shared decision-making process by developing a good working relationship with the Office Manager as described in 5.

7. To ensure that all assigned office equipment is maintained in proper working order for the smooth operation of Clerical Services.

c. Self-development Program

1. By March 31, 1992, to develop a working knowledge of Wordperfect through available manuals and reference books.

2. To develop written and verbal communication skills through supervising staff, seeking counsel, reading reference material and attending seminars.

3. To develop supervisory skills through supervising staff, seeking counsel, reading reference material and attending seminars.

4. Through self-directed and directed learning, to stay up to date on issues related to Clerical Services (office equipment, automation, personnel and supervision) so as to offer timely and topical advice to the Office Manager.

forms used by many companies often don't fit the job that is being evaluated. The result is performance appraisals that are, at best, less useful than they could be, or, at worst, frustrating experiences for both employees and their managers.

Well-designed performance plans, on the other hand, provide a custom tool for evaluating performance according to the specific objectives of each particular job; objectives that both the employee and the manager have been aware of throughout the year. They spell an end to those dreaded "surprises" at performance evaluation time.

For employees, the incentive to accomplish more comes from pride in their job and in the company. A performance plan that includes employee input will also have the employee's commitment to achieve the expected results. A thoughtful, personal performance plan gets employees involved and shows them the importance of their contribution.

A performance plan might have changed the ending of the lobster-mobile story. If Howard Hughes had provided his experts with more direction and a fuller picture of his visionary project, he might have had the pleasure of putting his steam-powered car on the road safely. After all, the technicians he hired were the best. But because Hughes gave so little direction and left out the essential information that safety was a priority for the car, the project was doomed to failure in spite of the sophisticated skills of his employees.

Case study: Dick, Gerry, and Tony

Dick has just completed his first year as a manager. He is a good performer, but he has some difficulties dealing with people. He supervises six employees, most of whom had been his peers. One of his subordinates, Production Supervisor Gerry, is four years from retirement. Gerry is in good health, competent and friendly, but he works at a relaxed pace. His productivity problem means that his department sometimes fails to meet deadlines.

Dick has done little to solve the problem because he has no clear-cut strategy for motivating Gerry. In fact, Dick finds the situation embarrassing because, although he likes managing, he realizes that he has a tendency to avoid rather than face such problems.

Another problem that Dick faces is with Tony, his engineering supervisor. Tony is considerably younger than Gerry, and everyone knows that Tony wanted Gerry's job. Tony felt he deserved the promotion instead of Gerry. Since Gerry's promotion, Tony has been polite to Dick, but his work has fallen off significantly. Things are getting worse as the two young estimators who work with Tony are also slacking off.

Dick has not discussed the situation with Tony, even though the problem is evident to everyone. Again, he simply doesn't know how to approach the problem, and he is embarrassed by his inadequacy.

Let's stand back and itemize the sources of the problem. Gerry and Tony are drifting because —

(a) job expectations are not clearly stated,

(b) there are no specific, measurable standards by which to evaluate their productivity, and

(c) Dick is reluctant to deal with the problems because he doesn't know how.

The list clearly suggests that performance plans for both Gerry and Tony could be just the solution Dick needs.

Working together on performance plans means everyone will become aware of the problems while taking positive steps toward solving them.

Confident that the performance plan is the right tool for dealing constructively with the issue of poor performance, Dick can concentrate on the important specifics. What key result areas should Gerry's performance plan include? What key result areas should Tony's include? How much time should he allow for the benefits of the performance plans to become evident?

Key results in the performance plan for Gerry should probably include the following:

- Production targets and time schedules
- Quality control guidelines
- Cost control targets
- Labor relations guidelines

Key results in Tony's performance plan would likely include the following:

- Preventative maintenance goals
- Construction target goals
- Contractor relations guidelines
- Equipment design specifications
- Machine operating standards

The positive results of the performance plans should be evident in six months. If six months pass with no evidence of change, Dick should reassess his own performance as a manager.

3. Developing a performance plan

Once you have explained the overall aims and uses of performance plans, ask your employees to take the first step in designing their own personal performance plans. Help them to begin by asking them to fill in a worksheet under the following column headings:

(a) Key results and reasons for priority

(b) Need or priority and measure of importance (percent or point value)

(c) Targets (results expected)

Sample #4 shows one way this could be set up as a worksheet for your employees and how it might be completed by an employee.

Some jobs are more difficult to measure than others, but none is impossible to measure. The first step in breaking down a job into its component parts is to identify separate areas of responsibility and accountability.

Key result areas are areas of responsibility for which specific goals can be prepared. For example, a key result area might be production scheduling, while specific goals for this area could include things such as meeting the production startup dates, maintaining customers' orders backlog to within five working days, not losing existing customers due to late delivery, etc. Key result areas are those major job components for which the employee is accountable.

After determining the key result areas — perhaps five for each job — the next step is to schedule a meeting with the employee to ensure that both of you agree on the key result areas, their priority and reasons for their priority, assessment of targets (i.e., how improvement in results will be measured). You and the employee can develop an action plan giving specifics such as who will review the purchasing policy and bid specifications by what date. The plan may go through a number of revisions and versions before it is satisfactory to both of you. During this process, keep the following points in mind:

(a) Ensure that targets of the performance plan are within the capabilities of the employee.

(b) Provide advice and direction to help structure meaningful commitments

(c) Determine how well the targets in each performance plan address the highest priority needs of the job at this time.

SAMPLE #4
PERSONAL PERFOMANCE PLAN WORKSHEET

Worksheet for_____

Key results and reasons for priority	Priority and percent share	Targets
Scheduling Backorders are causing loss of customers	Priority 1 (33%)	Starting dates met. Maintain backlog to max. 5 work days. Customers retained.
Cost control Material and indirect labor costs too high	Priority 2 (27%)	Reduce material costs Maintain direct labor cost; Eliminate indirect labor cost.
Supplies and high inventory Production delays caused by late receipt of supplies	Priority 3 (20%)	Eliminate production delays due to supplies. Control inventory to within 10%.
Safety Lost time due to accidents increased by 5% in last period	Priority 4 (15%)	Reduce hours lost due to accidents. Reduce insurance (workers' compensation) cost. Reduce number of unsafe conditions.
Security It is suspected that inventory loss is caused by theft.	Priority 5 (10%)	Eliminate employee theft. Reduce inventory loss by 50%.

Employee name_____

Performance plan for the period _____

(d) Assess how the targets for your subordinates support and reinforce the targets of your own performance plan.

(e) Evaluate how realistic the performance plans are relative to the problems that stand in the way.

The meeting between you and the employee to develop the performance plan is very important, so plan it carefully, establish a cooperative atmosphere, and be sure that you receive a commitment for the performance plan. When the meeting is over, don't forget to thank your employees for their share in the work and tell them that you will be monitoring their progress with interest.

Don't forget to set a good example by developing a high-quality performance plan for yourself with the help of your boss.

As you create and revise performance plans for all of your employees, use the following checklist to ensure that they contain the essential ingredients.

(a) Has the necessary information been assembled?

(b) Have the expected key results for the job been identified and listed?

(c) Have the key results been prioritized?

(d) Have potential obstacles been identified?

(e) Have realistic targets been set for each key result area?

(f) Have the appropriate measurements been specified, such as quality, quantity, time, cost?

(g) Does the performance plan adequately address accountability?

(h) Have all key people who can affect the outcome been involved?

4. Follow-up

Because change is a constant fact of life, performance plans need to be monitored and adapted regularly. Consider the need to revise performance plans as an opportunity to encourage your employees to determine what is wrong and develop actions plans to solve the problems. Interim review meetings at least once each quarter provide the appropriate setting for rethinking the performance plan. As part of routine follow-up, you should —

- provide regular feedback on performance plans;

- schedule regular interim follow-up meetings (at least once per quarter) to check progress toward targets;

- ensure that all team members are aware of their coworkers' individual commitments, and encourage a cooperative, helpful attitude among team members;

- encourage employees to be innovative, developing solutions for any obstacles they encounter in achieving their performance plan targets;

- create opportunities to discuss with employees their progress as well as the obstacles they are facing;

- analyze all performance plans that are in trouble to determine why they are faltering and what can be done to improve them; and

- keep in mind that *all* the tasks in your employees' performance plans must be completed for you, the manager, to achieve your objectives.

d. SUMMARY

To be an effective manager you must provide job orientation and ongoing direction for your employees. Employees who know they are doing what's expected of them have high job satisfaction and work well. As manager you must —

(a) provide new employees with a clear set of objectives for their job;

(b) show new employees the best alternatives for reaching these objectives;

(c) in cooperation with each employee, design a detailed performance plan for each job to provide ongoing direction for each employee;

(d) use the performance plan as the standard for evaluating the employee's performance; and

(e) revise performance plans regularly.

To learn more about performance plans, read *Personal Performance Contracts — The Key to Job Success* by Roger Fritz.

Encourage employees to be innovative

4

STEP THREE:
DESIGNING THE WORK ENVIRONMENT

For most of the 1970s, I managed a company that produced and marketed components for industrial machinery. It was then that I first became aware of what the work environment means for workers' comfort and productivity. As a responsible manager, I jumped right in with enthusiastic improvements to the workplace.

Having read somewhere that the addition of music would create a calming influence, I arranged for a system to pipe music to both the office and the plant. However, some time later when I visited the plant, I was struck by the quiet. The music wasn't playing there even though it sounded fine in the office area. Searching for a defect in the system, I discovered that the plant workers had stuffed rags in the speakers to silence them. They had found listening to the "white noise" day after day irritating rather than soothing.

Interestingly enough, I had chosen not to have the music piped into my office, so I had no experience of the long-term effects of the music. Without really thinking about it, I had exercised control over my work environment. The employees who muffled the system to shut out the invading noise had also taken control of their environment, and rightly so.

They taught me an essential truth that day: employees know best the conditions under which they work best. Therefore, it is essential that they be involved in any decisions made about their workplace.

I have since learned that in the 1960s research had already been done on the stressful effects of unwanted noise. Experiments conducted by researchers at Cornell University revealed that while music may be a pleasant accompaniment to routine, everyday tasks, it may interfere with more demanding, problem-solving work. Music is "digested" by the right side of the brain, while routine tasks are controlled by the left side of the brain. Original thinking, however, involves the right side of the brain — and the right brain can't solve problems very well when it is also occupied listening to music.

As the employees in my plant discovered, problems requiring right-brain thinking arise on even the most routine jobs. Music then becomes irritating and distracting. In fact, piped music could even mean that an original solution to a job-related problem is lost forever.

As I learned that day walking through a quiet plant, a manager's good intentions don't necessarily assure a comfortable and productive workplace. Knowledge based on research and experience is also essential to avoiding sometimes-costly mistakes.

To help you make sensible decisions about your workplace, both theory and case studies about workplace conditions are discussed in this chapter.

a. WORKPLACE CONDITIONS AND PRODUCTIVITY

A satisfactory work environment is neither a luxury nor a status symbol. It is a necessity for assuring happy, productive employees. When work conditions are poor, people grind away at their tasks without the spark of motivation. Productivity slides, and the best people inevitably leave.

In their book *Peopleware*, Tom De Marco and Timothy Listen make the point very clear. In analyzing projects in the computer industry, they found that, on average, 15% of all

When conditions are poor, people grind away at their tasks without the spark of motivation

projects are either canceled or aborted. The odds for large projects are even worse, with 25% of large projects (those requiring more than 25 work years) never completed. Surprisingly, the causes of these expensive failures are not technical ones. The researchers discovered that the work environment created the problems behind the failed projects.

The bottom line is this: either you pay for work-conducive space when you design and redesign the workplace, or you pay for it in lost productivity. Because better performers naturally gravitate toward organizations that provide a better work environment, the cost of the second option is probably many times the cost of the first. Your best people are your company's best resource, and a good work environment is high on the list of desirable features that attract good employees.

b. ESSENTIALS OF THE WORK ENVIRONMENT

The work of architect and philosopher Christopher Alexander provides useful guidelines for designing comfortable workspaces. In a three-volume series entitled *The Timeless Way of Building*, he and his colleagues at the Center for Environmental Structure set out the elements of good architectural design — design that balances the needs of the individual and the needs of the whole.

For example, in a section on "Workplace Enclosures," they note that people cannot work effectively in a workspace that is either too enclosed and confining or too exposed. A good workspace strikes a balance between enclosure and exposure. Placing people in relation to walls is also important. People feel more comfortable in a workspace with a wall behind them, and if there's a blank wall in front of them, it should be no closer than eight feet. If the wall in front is too close, workers can't rest their eyes by looking up, since the eyes can't change focus.

Alexander also makes some useful points about noise. He says that people concentrate better when they can't hear noises very different from those they make themselves, and when people around them are doing the same thing they are doing. Thus workspace should be arranged to eliminate "foreign" noise and to put together people with similar tasks, making similar noises. People who work with word processors, for example, should be grouped together, as should people who frequently use the phone.

In short, to do their best, people require adequate space, quiet, privacy, and control over their environment. But just how these principles are best applied to the needs of any particular plant or office design will vary considerably from workplace to workplace. In planning workspace design and changes, effective managers ask these questions:

- What kind of space and layout would support our workers best, making them comfortable and productive?

- What conditions would make our workers feel best about themselves and their work?

These open questions are a tool you can use to get all affected workers involved in decisions about their own workspace. As I have learned — sometimes through mistakes — they know their own needs better than anyone.

The work environment is more than just workspace. Space, layout, and noise are only a few of the elements of the work environment that affect productivity. The other factors are usually negatively defined as work obstacles. Here are some examples of work obstacles that prevent people from doing their best work —

- Illness or bad weather

- Inadequate tools

- Lack of material to process

- Insufficient budget

- Equipment breakdown

- Problems with fellow workers

The manager's first job is to identify the problem and isolate the cause. Once work obstacles are identified, managers can consider solutions. Even when the problem seems beyond anyone's control, there is usually some action which can at least minimize the negative effects on workers and their productivity. For example, even the most experienced managers can't control weather and illness. But they can have emergency or back-up plans in place to reschedule work or allocate it to other workers when necessary.

c. PERSONAL CONFLICTS

1. Understanding conflict

One of the main disrupters of work is conflict between people. Interpersonal differences often become most pronounced when the stakes are high, but every organization has its share of small issues blown into major battles.

Whether the conflict is openly hostile or subtle and covert, it involves strong personal feelings. Few managers know how to deal effectively with interpersonal conflict, yet the ability to manage conflict is critical to managing successfully.

Whether the conflict is openly hostile or subtle and covert, it involves strong personal feelings

As a manager, the first thing you need to understand is that conflict between people is an organizational reality and is neither good nor bad in itself. It can be destructive, but it can also be productive.

For example, a manufacturing manager may get angry enough at being pushed around by the vice-president of sales that she decides to try harder to produce a workable production schedule — just to show that she can do it! Interpersonal conflict sometimes clarifies persistent, underlying organizational problems that are finally addressed because they can no longer be smoothed over. Conflict can also give the participants a better understanding of their personal values, or force managers to clarify and articulate their ideas more effectively as they act as intermediaries.

The potentially destructive side of conflict usually dominates when conflict is either suppressed or allowed to escalate uncontrollably. The result tends to be dramatic and emotional upheaval for those involved. Careers may be sidetracked or ruined. Lost productivity and bad decisions may affect the entire organization. The irony is that people determined to win their battles often cause major losses both to themselves and their organization.

2. Dealing with conflict

Good managers give priority to solving their people problems first. They know it's important to take steps not to avoid conflict, but to prevent its destructive consequences. When faced with interpersonal conflict, they ask themselves the following:

(a) What are the likely effects of the conflict on the organization?

(b) What are the behavior patterns of the parties? What do they reveal about the issues, perceptions, underlying causes?

(c) What are the major issues in the conflict? How are the issues perceived by each party?

(d) What are the background conditions that led up to the conflict?

50

(e) What objective third party, inside or outside the organization, might act as intermediary?

The next step is mediation — a method by which someone not involved in the conflict helps the parties to reach an acceptable solution. You, the manager, or some other third party may act as mediator. The mediator's job is to find a resolution that all parties accept. (Forcing a win-lose situation, where one party wins at the expense of the other, is not mediation.)

The role of mediator requires skill and patience as well as persistent efforts to get the parties to listen to one another. Throughout the process, the mediator is constantly on the lookout for compromise solutions. Here is a list of the necessary qualifications for an effective mediator:

(a) Impartiality — to be credible, a mediator must not favor any party, or be too close to either party.

(b) Objectivity — strong opinions, likes, and dislikes undermine a mediator's role.

(c) Maturity — mediators must be able to keep their feelings and opinions to themselves. Above all, they must refrain from discussing the situation with any other employee, regardless of rank.

(d) Sensitivity — they must respect the feelings of the parties.

In some cases, a mediator can resolve conflict quite quickly by suggesting ways to alter the conditions that feed the conflict. Solutions might be as simple as extending deadlines, modifying departmental policy, allowing temporary exceptions, or setting up regular information meetings.

When mediation fails to ease or resolve the conflict, the only option left is controlling. In extreme cases, controlling means transferring or firing one of the parties. More often, however, it means some or all of the following:

- Reducing or preventing the interaction of the parties
- Structuring their interaction
- Changing the external pressures

Controlling may be the only option when there is a power imbalance between the parties; when one party can dominate by exerting pressure on the other.

The following three case studies dramatize typical conflicts and illustrate the appropriate means of resolving them.

Case study #1: Conflict between departments

Hank, a product manager, and Petra, an inventory control manager, would meet regularly to review and update sales forecasts. They held equal rank in a mid-sized company. Their interests inevitably conflicted somewhat, since Hank wanted to minimize unit costs and avoid stock-outs, while Petra wanted to minimize total purchasing costs and inventory levels. On several occasions when their forecasts proved to be inaccurate, the two managers had strong disagreements over forecasting procedures and goals.

Several conflicts later, each manager lost sight of the other's basic assumptions and roles within the organization. They began to personalize their differences, each feeling threatened and attacked by the other. As their personal antagonism and distrust intensified, they saw ulterior motives and unpleasant personality traits in one another's behavior. They began calling each other names, accusing one another of stupidity, self-interest, and even dishonesty. What had started out as a legitimate set of differences transformed itself into an emotional battle.

Mediation is the solution here. Since the parties are of equal rank and the different interests are built into their jobs, the situation can't be controlled by changing the work process or transferring one to another job. Moreover, this mid-sized company would likely have a human resources department with personnel trained to act as mediators.

Case study #2: Power imbalance

John is on the order desk at an engineered products manufacturing company. In fact, John *is* the order desk, since he is the only person who processes telephone inquiries and orders. He backs up three sales engineers who sell to manufacturers and distributors.

While John has a sound knowledge of the company's products and their application, he tends to be somewhat terse with customers. For example, he's quick to tell them that they "can't use this product this way" or that they "haven't selected the proper size for their purpose." Naturally, when customers complain to the sales engineers about John's manner, they become annoyed with him, especially when a customer chooses a competitor's product as a result of John's behavior.

When the facts are reviewed internally at company meetings, it always turns out that John was right in his assessment. The sales engineers nevertheless insist that John modify his approach by suggesting that the sales engineer visit the customer rather than by telling the customer what's what.

After repeated and unproductive sessions with John and his boss, who is the office manager, the sales engineers appeal to the general manager. Because the company is relatively small, the general manager doubles as sales manager and supervisor to the three sales engineers.

The general manager meets with John and the office manager and clearly explains that being technically correct is not the issue. The issue is John's manner with customers. Moreover, advising customers is not John's responsibility but that of the sales engineers. They know their clients and can "handle" them appropriately.

The situation does not improve despite the general manager's repeated interventions. Customers continue to complain or report controversies with John. He seems unwilling to change.

In this case, the general manager has tried to act as mediator. She has failed and no other mediator is available in this small company. Controlling by either changing the situation or replacing the parties is the only possible solution. The situation could be changed by having John report to the general manager in her role as sales manager. Then she would supervise John directly rather than through the office manager.

However, the disadvantages of this plan make it likely to fail. Such a move would mean separating order processing from inventory control — two functions that require close coordination. Furthermore, this option would leave John unsupervised during the long periods when the general manager's multiple responsibilities take her away from the office.

After weighing all the options, the general manager tells the office manager to terminate John's employment and to find a person with stronger interpersonal skills for the position. This solution is preferable to that of removing the three sales engineers.

Case study #3: Work tools

Rose is a hairdresser in a downtown salon which employs four other full-time stylists as well as several part-time ones. She feels that she has lost her professionalism because she has been hiding her tools from Eddie, a light-fingered coworker. Rose keeps her tools organized and in the proper place, but Eddie isn't so tidy. If he can't locate his own scissors, he'll grab Rose's and then forget to return them. Rose feels that she's being selfish and childish in hiding her tools, but she also knows that it's the only way to ensure they're there when she needs them.

This case is a classic one of disruptive behavior in the workplace. It shows how people can work themselves into a tizzy about little things. If the employee dealt directly with the issue, it might well solve the problem. However, the situation has gone on for so long that Rose feels that she can't talk to Eddie, partly because Eddie doesn't even realize there's a problem. Rose hasn't complained to management because she fears that it might leave ill feelings and because she feels guilty about not having confronted Eddie herself. She finally tells her supervisor what has been going on.

Experts usually recommend that employees deal face to face with coworkers' annoying habits, since they don't usually involve the company's operations. They advise thinking through the wording so that the coworker gets the message in the least offensive manner. In this case, however, the supervisor must intervene as mediator since Rose is reluctant to talk to Eddie herself.

The supervisor should make it clear to both parties that the problem is not serious and that she is not acting as an enforcer. She is there to help Eddie understand that his behavior annoys Rose. Mutual adjustments made by both parties are far better solutions than enforced changes.

During a frank mediation discussion among all three, Rose may well discover that some of her habits also annoy Eddie. An open, non-threatening mediation session may thus give the opportunity for addressing and solving more than one problem.

d. SUMMARY

Managing the work environment is the third step in an effective management style that puts people first. A work-conducive environment is a necessity. It guarantees greater productivity and a lower turnover, especially among your best people. To maximize the quality of your work environment, keep the following in mind:

- The work environment is defined by space, physical layout, noise, tools, materials, and relationships with coworkers. The quality of all of these has a significant positive impact on the quality of the work produced.

- Since workers themselves know which conditions help them work their best, they should be given a strong voice in decisions affecting their work environment.

- Workspace should strike a balance between exposure and confinement.

- Noises should be limited to those that are natural to the workplace itself. Employees doing similar work should be grouped together.

- Obstacles to work should be removed as quickly as possible; better still, managers should try to anticipate and prevent them.

- Interpersonal conflict must be managed and resolved. Mediation should be tried first. If mediation fails, then managers must solve the problem by controlling the situation or the people involved.

Try Worksheet #3 now and see how you currently deal with work environment problems and other conflicts.

WORKSHEET #3
DESIGNING THE WORK ENVIRONMENT

Consider you current position and the employees who report to you. Then, ask yourself these questions:

1. Have I given my employees any say in the design and layout of their workspace?

_____

2. Do I allow my employees to alter their workspace, or do I insist they leave things as they are?

_____

3. Do I allow my employees to "personalize" their workspace, or do I insist that only company-related items be used to decorate the workspace?

_____

4. Do I always deal with obstacles that prevent my employees from working at their best and most efficient?

_____

5. Do I tend to ignore interpersonal conflict in the area under my control? Or, realizing the importance of dealing with such conflict quickly and appropriately, do I follow the three steps to resolve conflict?

_____

(Step 1: clarifying the issues. Step 2: mediating, if possible. Step 3: controlling.) If your answer to any of these questions is negative, you need to refine your skills in these areas — knowing when to share control and when to take control.

5
STEP FOUR:
APPLYING TRAINING
AND SKILLS DEVELOPMENT

a. TRAINING FOR THE FUTURE

Training, the foremost human resources magazine in North America, has been tracking how much money U.S. companies have been spending since 1982 in training their employees. Here are some of the highlights of a report published in the October, 1990 issue:

- Total amount budgeted for formal training: $45.5 billion.

- Total number of people who have received employer-sponsored training: $39.5 million

- Total number of training hours: $1.3 billion

- Total amount budgeted for outside expenditures, such as seminars and packaged training programs: $9.2 billion

- Types of organizations with the highest average expenditures on training: transportation, communication, utilities

- Type of employee likely to get the greatest amount of formal training: salesperson

No matter how you look at it, the U.S. organizations polled in this study are spending an average of $1,152 per employee on training. To put it another way, the expenditure for employer-sponsored training in 1990 amounted to about

$400 for every person employed in the United States! The amount of money devoted to training employees is growing at a rate of about 12% per year.

While outlays for training are not yet so hefty in Canada, both the federal and provincial governments are promoting "training cultures" among Canadian companies. These governments, as well as others in the business community, anticipate that North America will play a "high-tech" rather than a manufacturing role in the coming global economy. So North Americans require training to prepare them for jobs demanding more sophisticated skills.

At a conference in Toronto sponsored by the *Financial Post*, speaker Thomas d'Aquino, president of the Business Council on National Issues, supported training development. He stated that "A skilled and adaptable work force is the key to a competitive advantage, and it should begin with the chief executive." In his view, "CEOs determined to keep their work force competitive should take the lead themselves by designating themselves 'chief educational officers' in the same way many have already added 'chief environmental officer' to their titles." D'Aquino argued that, in addition to work-specific skills, employees should be taught, for example, how their work affects the environment. Employees also need more training in interpersonal skills.

At the same conference, Dennis Williams, chairman and chief executive officer of General Electric Canada Inc., told the audience that the company's U.S. parent organization spends $500 million worldwide each year on education and training as a "strategic investment." He added that the money spent today on training gets far better mileage than the money spent on automation in the 1980s in a failed attempt to boost productivity.

It's certainly clear from these reports and comments that a great deal of money is being spent training employees. The money is targeted not only for skills development but also general education. It's also clear that the money is being spent with the firm expectation that more training will mean more "high-tech" output.

Unfortunately, the harsh reality is that experts estimate at least half the money spent on training is wasted. This chapter explores the reasons for this waste and shows you how to cut losses and make training both effective and cost-effective.

b. IS TRAINING REALLY THE ANSWER?

First, we need to clarify just what "training" means. Training means helping people to acquire job-related skills, skills that either make employees more productive in their current work or prepare them for more difficult jobs. Learning a skill without putting it to work on the job means simply acquiring knowledge. While there's certainly nothing wrong with acquiring knowledge, it shouldn't be confused with skills training. A skill is not a skill unless it is actively practiced in real job situations. One of the major causes of wasted training dollars is that the skill learned at company expense is never applied on the job.

Why would employers spend money training employees in skills they won't use? When training gets used as the all-purpose solution to any and every performance or productivity problem, waste is certainly inevitable. Such misuse of training is one of the built-in dangers of a "training culture."

Before skills training is proposed as a solution, the manager must determine that a skills deficiency is really the cause of the problem. If the problem is caused by having the wrong person in the job, training won't solve it. If the problem is caused by lack of orientation to the job, or poor tools to work with, training won't solve it. In short, the all-too-common practice of applying training to solve productivity problems is equivalent to throwing money away. Skills training can solve a problem only when the problem is the result of skills deficiency.

The following story vividly illustrates this point. A large distribution center for a retail organization loaded and shipped 15 to 20 truckloads of merchandise to its 600 stores every day. But the goods were often ruined by the time they arrived at the stores. Lamp shades were crushed under heavy cartons of hardware, and paint cartons loaded upside down leaked paint over what was stacked beneath. The operations manager at the distribution center decided that the solution was to train the loaders to load the trucks properly. Everyone was frustrated and confused when the amount of goods destroyed increased rather than decreased after the training.

A management consultant was called in to improve the training program for the loaders. Before refining the training, the consultant decided to define the problem. On paper, the loading process looked sensible and trouble free:

(a) The merchandise for each store was prestacked for loading in the warehouse.

(b) A conveyor carried the merchandise to the back of the truck for loading.

(c) Two employees inside the truck took the merchandise off the conveyor and stacked it from floor to ceiling.

(d) These loaders were trained to sort and load merchandise appropriately according to weight, size, type, etc.

However, when the consultant watched the loading in action, the real problem became evident. To maintain speed in loading the trucks, no one except the foreman was permitted to slow down or stop the conveyor. Truck loaders were actually grabbing and loading cartons as they came off the conveyor in rapid succession, with no time to sort the merchandise.

The problem was not the loaders' lack of skill but the unalterable speed of the conveyor. Loaders had no time in which to apply the skills the company had spent so much on enhancing. So the problem here was created by the work environment, and no amount of employee training could rectify it. Once the problem was isolated, the solution was simple and inexpensive: install a shut-off switch at the truck-end of the conveyor so loaders could slow the process when necessary.

c. FINDING SKILLS TRAINING THAT WORKS

Even when the problem has been accurately identified as a skills deficiency that can be corrected by educating employees, training may be ineffective. Training success must be measured by the number of employees who consistently apply their learned skills on the job. Yet many training programs in many companies just don't follow through on that crucial last step.

A typical training program looks good in theory:

(a) Before training, define the real problem, seek alternative solutions, select the most acceptable solution, commit to action.

(b) Develop a step-by-step training module; teach the steps in the classroom; ensure that all trainees understand each step; conduct role play and exercises so that everyone can practice each step.

(c) Have all trainees commit themselves to practicing these steps on the job so they can perform them smoothly and naturally. Instruct their bosses to encourage them to apply the skills on the job.

The problem with this program is that, while the trainees may have learned the steps involved in applying the skills, that is, they have acquired knowledge, they have not yet learned the skill. In the workplace, a skill is not a skill until it has become an integral, natural part of doing the job.

The program certainly encourages trainees to apply the skills on the job, but research into the effectiveness of training programs reveals that encouragement just isn't enough. Predictably, workers are more comfortable doing things the way they have always done them, whatever the disadvantages of the old methods. When they experience the inevitable difficulties and failures in trying a new way, they naturally revert to the old methods rather than persist in refining their new skills.

The experience of one training company illustrates that the degree of success achieved by training isn't always obvious. This company develops training packages for other organizations. Trainees seem to learn readily from their training presentations and client companies express a high degree of satisfaction with the training. To confirm these satisfying results, the training company conducted a follow-up to determine how well trainees transfer the skills to the job. To everyone's surprise, the follow-up revealed that only half of the trainees actually practice on the job the skills they seemed to develop so readily during training.

d. "SOFT-SKILLS" TRAINING

Another training and consulting company has taken care to clarify the important difference between the degree of success one can reasonably expect from technical or "hard-skills" training and "soft-skills" training.

Hard skills are relatively concrete, definable skills such as operating a machine, installing electrical wiring, framing a house, using an adding machine, or typing. These skills can be learned and improved by almost everyone and, after adequate practice, they become second nature to the person using the skill.

Soft skills are more complex and involve dealing with people. Judgment, deductive reasoning, tact, and negotiation fall into the category of soft skills. Hard skills can be applied uniformly in all situations requiring that skill; the use of soft skills must adapt to each person that you deal with.

Managing and selling are two areas that demand many soft skills. They are, therefore, good examples for analysis and study, including comparison. Managing means getting results through other people with their full cooperation. Selling is getting results through other people with their full cooperation as well. The difference is that managing concerns people in the same organization who report to you, while selling deals with people outside the organization who do not recognize the sales person to be in a position of authority over them.

One training company has this to say about transferring hard and soft skills to the job:

"The definition of a successful *technical training* program is one in which 90% of the trainees master 90% of the skills being taught—and transfer these skills to the job. *Soft-skills training*, on the other hand, is much more a hit-or-miss proposition. [In this case] we are lucky if 20% of the trainees who graduate from our courses go back to the job and actually use the techniques we taught them. The other 80% may try out their new 'skills' a few times, but then quickly revert to their old patterns."

My own experience of soft-skill training confirms this view: soft skills must be taught and reinforced again and again before trainees apply the new techniques on the job.

Accepting a more modest success rate for soft-skills training than for technical training does not mean that we can't still improve our batting average. As a manager, you can achieve the best possible success rate by ensuring that soft-skill training incorporates some or all of the following strategies:

(a) Use the "boss-is-the-trainer" method. Before training employees, train the boss in the new skills. Then instruct him or her in the best ways of training the employees and reinforcing their efforts on the job. With this method, employees can consult the boss as an on-the-spot expert when they encounter difficulties in applying the new training. They are less likely to fall back into old patterns.

(b) Repeat the training periodically until an acceptable number of employees apply the new skills on the job. This technique soon gets the message across to employees that the company is seriously committed to their using the new skills.

(c) Break down the training into a series of small steps. Practice each step until trainees "own" it before introducing the next one. Evidence shows that breaking down the training into a series of steps is essential for successful training in soft skills.

Practice each step until trainees own it

1. Step-by-step training

The step-by-step training method naturally requires a longer, slower training program than ordinary methods, but the benefits make it well worth the extra time. To better understand its benefits, consider the step-by-step method as it is applied in teaching someone to play golf. The first step is learning how to grip the club. The second is how to align the feet and shoulders. The third step involves how to swing the club and hit the ball squarely. The whole learning process may involve some 15 steps.

Even if you have never taken golf lessons, you can well imagine that a pro golf instructor would get nowhere fast by teaching you all 15 steps at one time and then expecting you to play a round, saving the critique until you completed the 18th hole! Such a method would guarantee only frustration and failure for both instructor and learner. In fact, golf pros teach only one step at a time, drilling trainees until they have mastered each stage before moving on to the next step. For example, new golfers are drilled in techniques for driving, putting, and escaping sand traps long before they ever play a complete game.

Just as in learning to play golf, in learning soft skills short, repeated drills of each step are the best way of developing and mastering new techniques. Drills also build confidence, and confidence is as important as mastery if trainees are to acquire a sense of "ownership" of the new skill. When trainees feel "ownership" of the new skills during the training program, the chances of their transferring them to the job greatly increase.

2. Applying soft skills to selling

A *Training* magazine survey states that over 50% of formal training is given to salespeople. This high percentage isn't surprising, since success in sales depends so heavily on a combination of several soft skills. Strong interpersonal, communication, and problem-solving skills are all essential to sales. This much-abbreviated account of the complex process of selling dramatizes the importance of step-by-step training, accompanied by extensive drilling at every stage to prepare salespeople.

Selling can be summed up as a four-step process:

(a) Sizing up the customer

(b) Planning a strategy

(c) Communicating with the customer

(d) Motivating the customer to buy

(a) Sizing up the customer

Sales are made to people, and each person is different. A potential customer may be tense, genial, hostile, wary, and so on. As soon as salespeople meet a potential customer, they must begin "sizing up" the person by asking themselves some questions:

(a) What is this person like?

(b) What characteristics must I deal with?

(c) What obstacles do I anticipate?

Strong skills in sizing up potential customers are crucial for salespeople, since success in all the subsequent steps hinges on their making an accurate initial assessment. Extensive training in applying Maslow's theory of personality types, discussed in chapter 2, and in other proven methods for assessing people, provides salespeople with critical tools for sizing up the customer. They can then determine the most appropriate ways of interacting with the person they want to sell to.

(b) Planning a strategy

Once salespeople have sized up the potential customer, they should ask themselves: What is the best way of dealing with this person? How should I overcome the obstacles I anticipate?

Strategy planning follows sizing up in the same way that a doctor's prescription follows the diagnosis. The salesperson lays out a plan of action designed to work best under the circumstances. Since Customer X is a different type from Customer Y, strategies will differ from customer to customer.

For example, a salesperson might size up Customer X as having a dominant need for security. That means the person says little, backs away from new ideas, shies away from discussing personal matters, likes routine, and is generally cautious. Through training and experience, the salesperson knows that the best strategy in this case is to quickly demonstrate that he or she is trustworthy, reliable, and willing to listen and cooperate. The salesperson would also want to demonstrate that the purchase involves no risk.

(c) Communicating

In communicating with customers, salespeople apply their strategy by choosing a communication style similar to that of the customer. For example, the best approach to the insecure customer would be one that is gentle and unpressured.

Yet salespeople know that all customers need answers to three questions before they will consider buying:

(a) What will this product or service do for me?

(b) Why should I spend money or time on it?

(c) What's in it for me?

It's likely that the quiet customer whose dominant need is security won't pose these or many other questions. In this case, the salesperson must also have the skills to anticipate questions and communicate answers without being asked directly.

(d) Motivating

Creating understanding by answering questions is not enough to make a sale. A successful sale requires the customer to act, to make the commitment to buy. The customer

GORILLA
DANGEROUS
Please not to approach
too close to the bars

Salespeople apply their strategy by choosing a communication style similar to that of the customer

who says, Thank you for the information, I'll think about it, or the employee who says to the boss, I know what you mean, and I understand what you expect, has not made a commitment.

A salesperson needs motivating skills in order to generate commitment from the customer. The customer needs a good reason to act. Salespeople provide this motivation when they demonstrate that the product or service will fill a customer's tangible or intangible need, preferably both. Tangible needs are measurable ones, such as the need for a reliable computer system. Intangible needs are psychological ones, such as the need for status or independence. Skills in assessing, responding to, and finally appealing to these often unspoken needs are essential to sales success.

e. FOLLOW UP

Training does not end when the course or session ends or when the training consultant goes home. Follow up is a most important part of the training process. Among other things, it tells you, the manager, how effective the training techniques were and whether the employee is able to apply the training to the job, and it helps the employee reinforce what he or she has learned.

After-training follow-up techniques include tests, short refresher seminars that support the earlier training, and, most important, observation by the manager. Managers should observe their employees closely to determine the extent to which each has transferred the learned skills to the job. The best time to correct and/or reinforce employees' skills on the job is when you, as manger, observe your employees. In order to do this, the manager must be an expert. This is why the "boss is the trainer" is such a vital concept. For the boss to be the trainer, he or she must learn the skills first before teaching them to the employee. After learning the skill and training the employee in it, the manager will indeed be the expert and ideally suited to correct or reinforce the employees as they go about their tasks.

f. SUMMARY

Good managers make sure that their employees get appropriate and effective training. Successful training requires an understanding of the training process and following a few guidelines:

(a) Training can solve a performance problem only when the cause of the problem has been correctly diagnosed and the training targeted as the cause.

(b) A skill is not a skill until it has been successfully transferred to the job.

(c) Employees are more likely to apply new skills on the job when they have "owned" the skill during training.

(d) Soft skills are complex skills such as tact, "reading" people, adapting yourself to other people, and judgment.

(e) Step-by-step training, including extensive drills at every step, boosts confidence as well as skill levels, increasing the likelihood that trainees will own and apply the skills.

Try Worksheet #4 and see how well you understand and apply training.

WORKSHEET #4
USING TRAINING EFFECTIVELY

Consider your current position and the employees who report to you. Then, ask yourself these questions:

1. How much of my budget is devoted to the professional development of my employees? How does this number compare with the U.S. average of $400 per employee annually?

_____

_____

_____

_____

2. Do I always do an analysis to determine the need for particular training before I commit to it?

_____

_____

_____

_____

3. When my employees have finished a training program, do I follow up to ensure that they actually apply on the job the skills they have been taught? What kinds of follow-up procedures do I use? List them.

_____

_____

_____

_____

4. Do I consider managing a "soft" skill — a skill even more complex than selling?

_____

_____

_____

_____

5. Selling and managing have both common elements and differences. List them.

Analyze your answers critically to determine whether you fully recognize the importance of focused training in improving the productivity of your people.

_____

_____

_____

_____

If you answered no to question 3, you know from reading chapter 5 that follow up is a very important stage of training. At this time, try to imagine some follow-up techniques that would help ensure that the money you spend on training is well spent.

If you answered yes to question 3, but were then unable to name tangible, quantifiable measures that you use to gauge success, you are fooling yourself into believing you do follow up. Unless the techniques you use are quantifiable, the follow up will be totally subjective and, thus, largely useless.

6

STEP FIVE:
MOTIVATING YOUR PEOPLE

In 1979, I made a career move, becoming president of a farm equipment company. I soon discovered a very disturbing problem: the people working in the plant were not motivated. They seemed to care little for the company, for the quality of its products, and even for their own jobs.

A vivid example of their negative attitude, and only one instance among many, came to my attention soon after my arrival. On at least one occasion, a punch press operator (whose job was punching holes in pieces of sheet metal) continued operating the press even after it became evident that the die had moved and the holes were being punched in the wrong places. He knowingly produced scrap for a large part of his shift.

At the time, I found the report of this incident hard to believe. I wondered how anyone could care so little about his or her work. The clear message was that the employee was not simply unmotivated or neutral, but completely de-motivated. The "will do" factors so essential to performing a job satisfactorily were wholly lacking in this employee and in many others.

What had gone wrong in this company that employees were so demotivated? How prevalent is this problem in companies today? What can be done to motivate employees? This chapter will explore these questions, and prepare you for the all-important task of motivating your people.

a. THE ROOTS OF DEMOTIVATION

One 1990 survey of Canadian organizations revealed that employees generally feel that their companies do not value the work they do. They feel frustrated on the job as a result. When employees were asked how the situation could be corrected, they replied that management should be better trained in people skills. Employees indicated that they expect to be valued as people and as workers. In practical terms, they want to be kept informed about decisions that affect them. Many said that managers hold back information in an effort to maintain power and control.

Additional information comes from a 1990 survey of 700 engineers in the United States. Nearly three-quarters of the engineers agreed that a poorly educated and poorly trained work force in the United States currently hinders productivity. More than half said that workmanship is worse than it was ten years ago. Sixty percent said that employees don't work as hard or as productively as they did in 1980.

When asked about the causes and attitudes behind falling productivity, 80% of the engineers cited the lack of a strong work ethic. Nearly all indicated that employees are not motivated at work, take less pride in their work and are less loyal than they used to be. They are not enthusiastic about their jobs and they resist change. When asked about solutions, fully 97% of the engineers indicated employee training, education, and motivation as essential ingredients in any plan to increase productivity.

The crux of the problem becomes evident in a 1990 survey of industrial companies with annual sales between $10 million and $200 million (so-called midsized companies). More than two-thirds of the 250 respondents noted productivity problems at their companies. What's especially interesting, however, is the response of the top executives of these companies.

When asked to describe the cause of the problem, 54% laid the blame on people, 27% blamed the process technology, and only 19% blamed plants and equipment. Yet when asked about their solutions to the problem, the most common answer by far was "increased capital investment," not, as one might expect, increased investment in people!

How can this be? Are North American executives so misguided that they can't see that people problems must be solved by investing in people?

The reality is that business executives do understand that capital investment won't solve the problem, but as Marshall A. Cohen, president and chief executive officer at the Molson Companies, believes, the reward system for executives effectively ties their hands.

In a 1990 speech, Cohen explained that the heart of the problem lies in the way executive success is measured and rewarded. Executives who produce big immediate profits receive the hero treatment, while executives who focus on long-term goals and growth receive pink slips.

Educating, training, and motivating a work force requires a long-term commitment. Yet North American executives can't make such commitments since their bonus and job security depends upon the next quarter's earnings. The pressure for short-term results comes from shareholders; more precisely, from institutional shareholders who want immediate profits. Their push for short-term profits is driving the North American market into shorter and shorter time frames.

In such a climate, long-term goals such as developing new products, opening up new markets, and educating, training, and motivating people naturally fall by the wayside. Executives lack the incentive to commit to any of these goals. We even lack a commonly accepted method for measuring success in these areas. Sadly, in North America, short-term profits have become our only measuring stick for both people and organizations.

Japan shows us that it doesn't have to be this way. Japanese executives aren't under the same high pressure to produce short-term profits. They can commit to long-term goals because of the concept of "patient capital." As stated, a great deal of the pressure for short-term profits comes from institutional investors. In North America, institutional investors provide the majority of investment capital, so short-term profits are the keyword. In Japan, institutional investors account for only a small percentage of the capital invested. The rest can be attributed to investors who are more interested in long-term gain, hence the designation "patient capital." Because these investors are not pushing for quick profits, this attitude can be passed on down to the management level.

b. PARTICIPATORY MANAGEMENT

A November, 1990 article in *Au Courant* makes it clear that it's people and not instant profits that will keep businesses competitive. It makes the point that how well we fare in the era of high technology depends critically on our capacity to work smarter. "Working smarter" means two things: the capacity to innovate, and a willingness to invest vigorously in developing our human resources. Innovative technology and human resources development are "the two steps forward that all — workers, businesses, labor unions and governments — must take if they are to have any hope of meeting the challenges of increasing competition on national and world markets, today and tomorrow."

While pointing to the solution, the article doesn't include specific blueprints, other than stating a basic principle: "People and organizations, no less than machinery and equipment, need constant care and upgrading." If North American businesses accepted this fundamental principle, half the battle against low productivity would be won.

The principle of caring for people means, first and foremost, creating a motivational environment, an environment in which employees want to do excellent work and are eager to learn how to do it. Such an environment is the product of a management philosophy that emphasizes quality in people-related functions: feedback systems, job evaluations, performance appraisals, job enrichment, consequences for good and bad performance, training and development, and employee expectations.

A *participatory management model* recognizes and meets the needs of today's employees and motivates people to do their best. Participatory management means that all employees, no matter what their job function, understand the mission and purpose of the organization as a whole. They see both "the big picture" and the way their own job fits into it. They are involved in decisions that affect their own work, and they are encouraged to bring forward their own ideas about how to do things better.

When employees have a voice in decisions and a vision of the role they play in the organization, they take pride in their performance. People who take pride in their work are highly motivated to perform at their very best.

My experience at the farm equipment company gave me first-hand experience of how a management style that puts people first turned a group of uncaring, unproductive employees into a productive team. Here's what we did:

(a) We organized regular meetings to keep employees informed about "the big picture." They learned about the company's products and the competition the company faced in the marketplace. They also learned that farmers' decisions to buy were often based on the reliability of the product rather than the price. They came to see that they were competing with competitors' employees to produce the best products at the most reasonable cost. Thus the company and the workers were together in the struggle for survival.

(b) At company expense, we took workers on farm visits to see first hand how the company's equipment was used and to demonstrate the importance of its trouble-free operation.

(c) We took plant workers to equipment shows, asking them to evaluate the equipment produced by our competitors, comparing it to our own products. We asked them for suggestions on improving our equipment.

It wasn't long before the quality of the company's products improved dramatically. Furthermore, the amount of scrap was reduced to near zero as workers took pride in making each component as near perfect as possible. The plant workers' involvement in decisions and their sense of participating in "the big picture" motivated them to pride and improved performance.

c. THE JAPANESE WAY

A look at management practices in Japan shows how some of the obstacles to productivity in North America might be overcome.

One major advantage Japanese companies have over North American ones is that their employees welcome technological change. By contrast, workers in North America often fight or attempt to sabotage such change. Workers on both sides of the Pacific have good reason for these very different responses. To the factory worker in North America, the introduction of labor-saving machinery may well mean jobs lost to automation. Japanese workers, by contrast, can depend on life-long employment with their company no matter what machines come along.

Furthermore, Japanese workers can count on higher pay and benefits when productivity increases. Increased company profits mean not only higher dividends for shareholders but also semi-annual bonuses for the workers. Bonuses are often worth four to six months' wages.

With life-long job security and strong incentives to productivity, it's no wonder Japanese companies have achieved such success in recent decades. Their secret is a close-to-ideal motivational environment.

In his book *The American Samurai*, J.P. Alston outlines the four axioms underlying the Japanese style of management. As you read them, you might note that North American businesses have assumed, historically, nearly the opposite:

(a) The worker who is capable of performing a specific job function is intelligent enough to improve the quality and productivity of the job.

(b) Given the opportunity, workers want to improve the quality of their work.

(c) Members of a corporation or company form a "family."

(d) The family group, that is, the company, is more important than the individual.

These principles are very simple. The first says that workers are not stupid. The second says that they want to do better. The third says that the organization, like a family, provides a sense of belonging and support, with all employees taking mutual responsibility for one another's well-being. Moreover, the individual owes loyalty to the company in exchange for employment. The fourth principle reflects the Confucian concept of the huge debt of gratitude and respect owed to parents and leaders (and bosses), one that can never be completely paid off no matter how long the relationship.

The abiding but non-contractual relationship between Japanese workers and their companies is summarized in the employees' creed recited by Matsushita employees every morning:

> Progress and development can be realized only through the combined efforts and cooperation of each member of our Company. Each of us, therefore, shall keep this constantly in mind as we devote ourselves to the continuous improvement of our Company.

d. APPLYING THE LESSONS

We certainly can't import Japanese management practices wholesale in an attempt to motivate North Americans. Our system is very different and Japanese business practices have deep roots in their very different culture. But managers in any company can apply some of these motivational strategies within their own departments.

1. Teamwork

Team spirit is one of the most striking aspects of Japanese companies. As a manager, you can create that team spirit among the people you supervise. Creating a team means creating a system of values, that is, a set of beliefs governing behavior, that employees are committed to support by deeds as well as words. A team working under a management style that puts people first would work together according to the following values:

(a) Full and free communication among team members regardless of rank or position.

(b) Reliance on consensus and shared decision making (as well as shared rewards) rather than on coercion.

(c) Influence based on technical competence, knowledge, and skill rather than personal whim or power plays.

(d) An atmosphere that permits and encourages personal and emotional expression as well as task-oriented behavior.

(e) A basically human bias, one that accepts the inevitability of conflict and is willing to cope with and mediate conflict.

Such values answer the basic human needs of people working together. When managers satisfy these needs, they create the motivational environment in which people work most productively.

2. Praise

It is well documented that personal praise from a manager is one of the strongest motivators, ranking even higher than cash rewards. To survive as a manager, use praise and recognition effectively and appropriately. The employees who consistently do satisfactory work deserve praise just as much as the few outstanding performers.

By recognizing satisfactory performance, you will reinforce your employees' commitment to doing good work. Ignoring satisfactory performance actually demotivates employees. They feel like they are working in a vacuum, not knowing whether their work is up to par.

The following list of "dos and don'ts" will help you use praise effectively and establish the atmosphere of trust in which praise is most meaningful.

Do —

- be sure that your employees know how you rate their performance; give recognition for consistently good work as well as outstanding work.

- enforce job performance standards; always being "nice" is not good management.

- help your employees to experience success, not failure, by setting challenging but attainable goals.

82

- plan carefully when you need to use discipline; give fair warning, be fair and objective, and discipline in private.

- make your expectations clear, and ensure that they are realistic.

- remember that you are influencing an employee's self-esteem every time you interact with him or her.

- be a leader as well as a manager.

Don't:

- encourage, even inadvertently, inadequate performance or inappropriate behavior.

- assume that employees know how you rate their work; tell them.

- reprimand employees on the basis of their "personality"; deal only with their performance and behavior.

- promise anything you may not be able to deliver; broken promises erode trust and motivation.

- try to be an expert in areas in which you aren't qualified; when you notice signs of problems outside your expertise (such as alcohol or drug abuse), direct employees to professional help.

- make careless comments and gestures; even inconsequential or unintentional ones may affect an employee's self-esteem.

e. MANAGING THROUGH LEADERSHIP

The last item in the "do" list says, "be a leader as well as a manager." There are times as a manager when you need not just management skills but leadership skills. For example, when a company or department faces major changes, a leader inspires employees with the extra energy and motivation they need to deal successfully with the challenges.

Discipline in private

Although some people develop both management and leadership qualities, the two functions are quite different. Managers are primarily organizers. Their task is to create human systems that can implement plans precisely and efficiently. They organize both the work and the people by staffing jobs with qualified people, communicating plans and goals to workers, delegating responsibility for specific tasks, devising systems for monitoring progress, and solving problems as they arise.

Leadership, on the other hand, involves coping with change by aligning people. Aligning people means gaining the commitment of many people to the new direction or vision. The leadership challenge, therefore, is essentially one of communication, to inspire and motivate people to move and keep moving in the right direction. By appealing to basic human needs, values, and emotions, leaders help people overcome the sometimes major obstacles that impede change.

Aligning always involves communicating with many more people than you would ordinarily talk to. The target population may include not only subordinates but also bosses, peers, and staff in other parts of the organization, suppliers, government officials, and even customers. Anyone who can help implement a vision — and anyone who could block its implementation — should be part of the leader's communication network.

Managing is not quite as exciting or glamorous as exercising leadership. The purpose of managing is to apply systems and structures to help people complete routine jobs day after day. But in most organizations, opportunities arise that demand leadership from managers — those bursts of energy that are necessary to keep moving in new directions according to a new vision.

When you assume a leadership role, you rely on motivation and inspiration to energize people. Motivating doesn't mean pushing them in new directions, but rather appealing to their basic needs for achievement, a sense of belonging, a feeling of control over their lives, and a desire to live up to ideals. To appeal to and satisfy these needs effectively, you need to apply specific leadership skills such as the following:

(a) Articulate and communicate the new vision in a way that confirms the values of the audience you are addressing.

(b) Involve people on a regular basis in deciding how to realize the vision and give them a sense of control.

(c) Support employees' efforts to realize the vision by providing feedback and coaching.

(d) Recognize and reward success.

When you are effective in these leadership tasks, the work itself becomes intrinsically motivating for employees.

Ian Percy, a management psychologist, eloquently summarized the difference between leading and managing in a 1990 speech:

> Managing is a form of superficial transformation; leadership is spiritual transformation — touching the heart of people. Every successful intervention into a human organization is spiritual intervention. Those who understand this possess magic; those who do not understand are limited to methodologies, i.e., managing.

f. SUMMARY

Creating a motivational environment through managing and leading is the fifth step in a management style that puts people first. Keep these crucial points in mind when you are seeking to improve motivation:

(a) Motivation has a direct effect on performance and productivity; unmotivated workers perform badly, and motivated workers perform well.

(b) Management philosophy and style create the motivational environment for people, since the management approach determines the consequences for good and bad performance and behavior.

(c) A people-centered management style, devoted to developing and caring for human resources, creates a highly motivational environment by satisfying basic human needs.

(d) Managers who are people-centered effectively use the tools of praise and team spirit to motivate their people.

(e) They work on developing their own communication skills so they are prepared to assume a leadership role when the need and opportunity arise.

Try Worksheet #5 and see how your current motivational strategies and leadership skills might be enhanced in order to promote productivity and encourage employees to see "the big picture."

Help your employees experience success

WORKSHEET #5
DO YOU CREATE A MOTIVATIONAL
ENVIRONMENT?

Consider your current position and the employees who report to you. Then, ask yourself these questions:

1. How would I rate the productivity of my employees compared to last year? To five years ago? To ten years ago?

_____

_____

_____

2. When I look at improving productivity, do I always consider both components for achieving it — innovative technology and human resources development?

_____

_____

_____

3. Do my employees know and understand the mission or purpose of our organization? Do they see how their own jobs contribute to the success of the organization?

_____

_____

_____

4. Do I include my employees in making decisions that affect their work? Do I encourage them to bring forward their own ideas for improvement?

_____

_____

_____

5. Do I look for opportunities to praise employees — not only star performers but everyone who does satisfactory work?

_____

_____

_____

In reviewing these questions, you will better understand that you, the manager, have the greatest influence in creating the motivational environment so important to productivity.

If your answer to question 4 is no, you realize now from reading chapter 6 that employees expect to be valued as workers. What better way is there to show employees that you value them than to ask them for their ideas and opinions about decisions that affect their work?

Employees will feel that companies do value them and their work when they are asked to contribute to decisions about the workplace. Unless you do include your employees in your decisions or at least keep them informed about your decisions, they will feel frustrated and demotivated.

7
PRODUCTIVE COACHING

For almost a decade, I was vice president of sales for an multinational company. The company, which marketed consumer products, had three sales managers heading three divisions, with each division responsible for three regions. Each regional manager supervised an average of six field representatives. Ensuring strong lines of communication up and down this pyramid of sales people was an important part of my job.

One situation typical of the ones I dealt with routinely, and typical of my management methods at the time, was miscommunication between one of the regional managers and his six field representatives. Some seemingly unrelated comments and events signalled a problem, but I couldn't tell just what it was.

At that time, I hadn't yet developed a management style that centered on people, nor did I know about the method of front-end analysis. So without any preliminary investigation of the causes of the problem, other than some hunches based on scanty information, I decided that a coaching session was the answer.

Since the regional manager didn't report to me directly, I decided to kill two birds with one stone by coaching him in the presence of his sales manager. This way, I could coach the regional manager and train the sales manager in coaching skills at the same time.

I started the coaching session by explaining that the purpose of our meeting was to come to an understanding of the problem and to address it for the benefit of both the people involved and the company as a whole. Then I asked the regional manager if he thought there was a communication problem between himself and his field representatives. He said that he wasn't aware of any. So I explained my reasons for believing that there was.

Working on some assumptions about what was wrong, I pointed out that, with a sales team scattered over a large area, the salespeople needed almost daily contact with their regional manager. His job was to initiate this regular contact so that everyone had the reassurance, support, and motivation that comes from the sense of being part of a team. An "open-door policy" was not enough; as regional manager, he needed to reach out, actively and regularly, to his people.

At this point, the regional manager explained that his method had been to write a long letter to each of his salespeople every month. After some discussion of this procedure, he could see that long monthly letters, including criticism of sales performance as well as information, could easily discourage free and open communication with his people. He readily agreed that people respond much better to immediate feedback, either positive or negative, than to formal, written letters itemizing a month's worth of comments.

We finished the coaching session by working out an action plan for the regional manager. The plan included making frequent phone calls to his people, dealing with problems as they occurred, and giving immediate feedback on performance. He would write letters only for conveying business information such as budgets, for giving formal recognition to achievements, and for issuing formal reprimands.

Looking back on that situation now, I'm simply amazed that we were able to identify and solve the problem in a coaching session. At no point did we ask ourselves about the cause of the problem, about why the regional manager was using this unusual method of communicating with his people, one they so disliked. If we had asked the question, we would have discovered the cause: this regional manager had been thrust into his management position with no orientation and little ongoing direction.

In other words, the root of the problem was a deficiency in providing orientation and ongoing direction. It was only later that I fully recognized not only this fundamental lack but also my guilt. As vice president of sales, I had neglected to provide the regional manager with the orientation, direction, and feedback he needed. If I had been a people-centered manager in those days, the communication problem would never have occurred in the first place.

Once I recognized my responsibility, I remedied the deficiency by providing the regional manager with solid orientation and direction. But it had really been only good luck that had made our first coaching session successful in solving the immediate communication problem.

a. WHAT IS COACHING?

The function of coaching is to correct relatively minor behavioral problems that may occur despite a "people first" management style. Coaching involves redirecting or changing wrong behavior, or reinforcing sound behavior. Coaching is not intended to correct deficiencies in managing according to the five basic steps.

In his book *Coaching for Improved Work Performance*, Ferdinand F. Fournier makes the crucial distinction between people and their behavior:

> As a manager, you will probably never become an expert on people although it is highly likely that you are already an expert on behavior. You are probably thoroughly familiar with the behavior that is appropriate for your subordinates in their specific jobs. START MANAGING THOSE BEHAVIORS.

Unlike training or performance appraisals, coaching is informal. Managers may coach whenever the need arises, sometimes even as the employee goes on with his or her work, without a scheduled meeting time or place. The sessions should last at most ten or fifteen minutes and deal with only one aspect of the job.

b. COACHING STEP BY STEP

Although coaching sessions are brief, the coaching process is important enough to your employees' performance to merit breaking it down into a series of steps. There are five steps to effective coaching:

(a) Open the discussion.

(b) Listen to the employee's views.

(c) Present your views.

(d) Resolve disagreements.

(e) Work out an action plan.

1. Open the discussion

At the very beginning, you want to make sure that the employee —

(a) doesn't feel threatened by the discussion with a superior, and

(b) is ready to participate in the discussion.

You can put people at ease by explaining the coaching process: its purpose, its potential benefits, and its ground rules (i.e., the five steps). Before plunging ahead, you should also make sure the employee is prepared to go along with you.

2. Get the employee's views

You usually go into a coaching session with at least some information about the issues you wish to address. But you should get the employee's views before giving yours. You

Make sure the employee doesn't feel threatened

may learn something you didn't already know that could alter your view or approach. Moreover, the employee should talk first so that his or her view of things isn't squelched or influenced by yours.

3. Present your views

When your views differ from those of the employee, explain what you disagree with and why. Be sure to avoid words and tones which might seem to belittle the employee. For instance, instead of saying, I don't care, say, It doesn't matter. Simply state the facts and summarize the points on which you agree and disagree. Be prepared for denial, defensiveness, or resentment, but don't go looking for it.

4. Resolve disagreement

At this point, suggest that both of you think and talk through your respective positions to find a compromise, a third position, that is more sound than either of the original ones. Pick the solution that promises to be most productive for everyone.

If no compromise is possible, you must impose your own solution. Explain it clearly and ask the employee if he or she thoroughly understands your decision.

5. Work out an action plan

Now you are prepared to work out the specifics of a work plan, indicating who does what, when, and where. Allow the employee to take the initiative in developing the plan. When the plan is complete, ensure that the employee understands it and is committed to making the requisite changes in his or her behavior on the job.

Even with the five-step approach, coaching is not easy. Most coaching situations involve some criticism of the employee's behavior or performance, and no one likes being criticized. That's why preparing for and organizing the coaching session is so important. When you have anticipated the employee's responses and questions, you are better prepared to deal with them. You then remain in control of the session, thus increasing the likelihood of a successful outcome.

c. COACHING FOR ATTAINABLE GOALS

Another requirement for a successful coaching session is setting a single clear, realistic, attainable goal for the employee. Employees will respond more readily to coaching once they see that you require only limited changes to their behavior rather than a major revolution. The following list presents such typical attainable goals. In any one coaching session, you would set only one of these goals:

- Completing reports on time (i.e., by a specific date)
- Writing more legibly
- Telephoning by a specific time each day

- Proofreading every report to reduce errors

- Communicating face to face rather than by memo for all but major reports

- Getting up a half-hour earlier to ensure arriving at work on time

- Limiting coffee/smoking breaks to five or ten minutes

- Using appropriate language

- Making no more than x personal phone calls per day

- Ensuring that criticism of employees is done in person and in private rather than by memo or in public

Keep in mind, as well, that it's unrealistic to expect startling, dramatic results from one coaching session. Coaching helps employees to improve by increments, small steps that build on each other.

d. COACHING FOR COMMITMENT

The most effective coaching sessions end in the employees making a real commitment to change. You can't always expect to get such a commitment, but you can work toward it in every coaching session.

The key to commitment is participation: the more initiative employees take in recognizing and solving the problem, the more committed they will be to changing. In coaching sessions, do all you can to make the process one of self-discovery for the employee. Get the employee to see the problem. Get the employee to articulate the goal. Get the employee to suggest how things might be changed. Get the employee to plan the specifics of the new work plan. It's only natural that people are ready to endorse wholeheartedly ideas that they come up with themselves, and not so wholeheartedly ideas that are imposed upon them.

Encouraging the employee to participate does not mean that you give up control. What you are doing, in fact, is using your authority to help people think for themselves. Most people do that better in a "safe" environment: one that provides guidance, encouragement, and structure. Coaching sessions can fill those needs exactly.

e. WIN-WIN RESULTS THROUGH ACTIVE LISTENING

In resolving any conflict between a manager and an employee, there are three possible outcomes:

(a) Manager wins, employee loses. This is the result when the manager imposes a solution and the employee agrees to change but doesn't really believe the change is necessary.

(b) Employee wins, manager loses. This is the result when the manager fails to convince the employee of the benefits of change and thus decides not to impose a solution, since such an effort would be futile.

(c) Manager wins, employee wins. This is the result when both manager and employee agree on a solution satisfactory and beneficial to both.

Achieving the third outcome, the "win-win" result, may require more time and more compromise than the other two. But the result is well worth the time and trade-offs. "Win-win" coaching is followed by a strong commitment from the employee, and means less effort is needed for you, the manager, to reinforce the solution. Furthermore, the parties to a such a solution feel good about their accomplishment and about each other.

On the other hand, an imposed solution may easily create resentment. People naturally resent those who exercise power to influence or change them. In fact, the more that

Get the employee to see the problem

managers use power, the less real influence they have over their employees.

To achieve that "win-win" scenario, use active listening. Active listening doesn't mean just listening to what the employee says. It means listening so that you can respond in ways that convey acceptance, thus encouraging the employee to go further into defining the real problem.

Usually, when employees begin discussing a problem, they are really talking about symptoms rather than the real problem, looking at the surface problem rather than the root problem. Through active listening, you can help them to explore further until they see and define the problem for themselves.

One of the keys to active listening is avoiding the natural tendency to moralize, judge, preach, and lecture. These reactions stifle rather than encourage open discussion and the employee's process of self-discovery. Be candid, but don't weaken your credibility by exaggeration. And never dampen his or her enthusiasm for the job or threaten the employee's self-respect. Rather than focusing on the employee's inappropriate behavior, you want to focus on the benefits a change in behavior will bring for the person. Emphasize the positives, such as improved teamwork, harmonious relationships, improved productivity, and especially increased opportunity for advancement.

The following do's and don'ts, examples of typical responses managers might make during coaching, illustrate the difference between the positive responses of an active listener and the critical responses that end open discussion:

Do say: It sounds like you feel as if you're being criticized from all sides.

Don't say: Come on. Accept what I'm saying as constructive criticism.

Do say: You're really feeling upset by his performance.

Don't say: He's under a lot of pressure these days.

Do say: You're afraid it might be too much for you.

Don't say: I know you can do it if you only try.

Do say: You're sorry now that you spoke up.

Don't say: You were obviously off base.

The atmosphere of acceptance and encouragement created by responses like these do's means healthy and positive interaction between the manager and the employee. In such a coaching session, there are no losers.

f. SUMMARY

Once you have satisfied the requirements of all five steps of a people-centered management approach, coaching is the method you use to solve employees' behavioral problems.

(a) Coaching means changing or redirecting an employee's behavior on the job. It is not intended to correct deficiencies in any of the five basic areas of managing.

(b) Coaching uses a five-step coaching process:

(i) Open the discussion.

(ii) Listen to the employee's views.

(iii) Present your views.

(iv) Resolve disagreements.

(v) Work out an action plan.

(c) To achieve the best results, your coaching session must —

- have a clear and attainable goal,

- be well prepared and organized, and

- take a "win-win" approach.

(d) As a manager, you need to follow a candid and open coaching style. Focus on the positive, and encourage the employee to take the initiative in thinking through the problem and solution.

(e) Don't expect miracles. Change takes time, and you must be willing to wait.

In his book *How to Improve Human Performance*, Thomas K. Connellan gives this very useful advice to managers that is particularly appropriate in the context of coaching:

- Avoid the fads, "cure-alls," and teaching gimmicks that suddenly appear on the scene, are hailed as panaceas, and disappear as abruptly as they appeared.

- Tolerate setbacks. There are no fool-proof techniques for developing employees. No matter how useful the method and careful the planning, setbacks are certain to occur now and then.

- Be patient. Changes rarely happen overnight. Changing habitual behavior is difficult, and the change process often takes place in stages so small as to be nearly imperceptible.

The long-term rewards are very real for managers who master coaching and are willing to wait for the results. They develop, over time, a team of cooperative, highly motivated employees who have good reason to trust the advice, opinions and goodwill of their managers. Now try Worksheet #6 and see how coaching fits into your current management style.

WORKSHEET #6
HOW ARE YOUR COACHING TECHNIQUES?

Consider your current position and the employees who report to you. Then, ask yourself these questions:

1. Have I ever tried to solve a problem through coaching without first determining the real cause?

_____

_____

_____

_____

2. Do I help employees find their own solutions to the problem?

_____

_____

_____

_____

3. Do I always prepare myself thoroughly before coaching an employee?

_____

_____

_____

_____

4. Do I begin coaching sessions by explaining the purpose and potential benefits of coaching?

_____

_____

_____

_____

5. Do I close coaching sessions by insisting on one single attainable goal from the employee?

_____

_____

_____

_____

Managing involves effective coaching to solve minor behavior problems before they mushroom and create problem employees and an unhappy department.

If you answered question 5 with a no, then your coaching sessions will almost certainly be a waste of time and effort. The purpose of a coaching session is to obtain a change in behavior on the part of the employee. Without an action plan and a commitment to this action plan by the employee, there is very little likelihood of the employee changing his or her behavior.

8
PUTTING IT ALL TOGETHER

When we speak of an employee's performance, what we are really talking about most of the time are the results of that performance. The quality of these results inevitably depends upon how well we, the managers, carry out the five steps. In this chapter, we'll look at how all of the steps work together to achieve every manager's dream: high-quality performance results.

a. HOW THE FIVE STEPS WORK TOGETHER

First, let's review our five steps from a new perspective:

1. Selecting the right people = WHO

2. Providing job orientation and direction = WHAT

3. Designing the work environment = WHERE/WHEN

4. Training and developing skills = HOW

5. Motivating = WHY

The virtue of these equations is that they provide a simple, easy-to-remember summary: Who does What, Where and When, How, and Why.

The equations also help us to see how the steps work in tandem. Two models simulate the interrelationships of the five steps.

1. Model #1

Results = Who + What + (Where + When) + How + Why

This formula adds the factors together, suggesting that the effect of the five steps is cumulative. If we assume 10 as the top rating for each step, then 50 is the maximum total for results. If one step is rated 5 while the others are rated 10, the results are 45, a decrease of only 10%.

This model presents a reasonable representation of the effect of deficiencies on productivity results. However, if a step were missing (rated 0), as in the case of an employee on sick leave, the results would still be as high as 40. This model, therefore, undervalues the effect of some kinds of deficiencies, but it is useful for illustrating how the five steps work together under some circumstances.

2. Model #2

The performance-results model shown in Sample #5 uses a graphic rather than mathematical mode of representation. It suggests that selection and placement of people, the box in the center, is the most important step. The model also illustrates that all of the steps or factors interact, but that they interact in no particular sequence. With no ratings assigned to the steps, the model implies that deficiencies in one step mean that the model is not "whole," and that the results will, therefore, be incomplete.

While this model lacks the quantitative precision of the mathematical model, it does demonstrate, in realistic terms, the interaction of all factors to affect the results.

b. IDENTIFYING THE CAUSE OF A PROBLEM

Model #2 also helps us to see very clearly that the root cause of a deficiency in results lies in one of the five areas, and that it is essential to isolate the cause in order to apply the correct, effective solution. For example, if a manager tries to solve a workplace problem with skills training, the results will not improve even though the employees have more skills. The model thus puts the appropriately strong emphasis on ana-

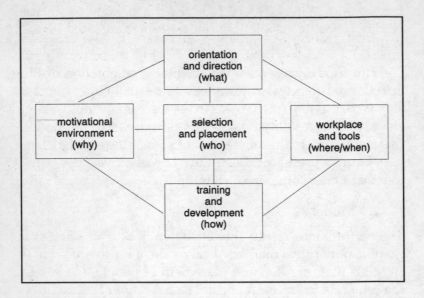

lyzing performance problems accurately so that the solutions will indeed improve the results.

I have made this point several times, in several ways, throughout this book. But it just can't be emphasized enough. In the sometimes complicated and rushed atmosphere of real-life managing, the temptation to "throw" a solution at a problem before taking the time to analyze the problem thoroughly is often very strong. As a manager, you must resist this temptation if you are to do your job efficiently.

Consider these typical answers to the question, Why is John performing so poorly these days?

- He needs a kick in the pants.

- We don't pay enough; what can you expect?

- It's hard to get good help these days.

- He's got a bad attitude.

- He must be having problems at home.

These answers are certainly familiar ones. They reflect all-purpose "gut-responses" that are all too often accepted without further investigation. And usually, the remedies applied are useless because they don't touch the real problem. Fortunately, the five-step model can help you get to the root of performance problems quickly.

c. IS THERE REALLY A PROBLEM?

Before you plunge into a complex and time-consuming analysis of the problem, first determine if the situation is serious enough to merit such efforts. You'll need to gather some basic information from four sources:

(a) Documents, including relevant data such as the employee's production levels, number of sales, sales margins, clientele, transactions, days absent, and so on.

(b) Discussion with the employee concerned.

(c) Discussion with others who know about the employee's performance.

(d) Observation of the employee performing his or her tasks.

On the basis of this information, you can usually judge whether the performance problem reflects an isolated incident or temporary lapse, or whether it's serious enough to require your time and attention. For example, managers shouldn't waste time investigating the reasons why an employee was late for work when the employee has not been late for over a year. And there's certainly no point in embarrassing a valued employee over a minor lapse that probably has no effect on overall performance.

In addition to determining whether it's worth your time, you must also decide whether the issue is important to the organization. The relative value of correcting the deficiency must be greater than the cost, in time and effort as well as money.

Finally, you should check to find out whether the employee is aware of the problem. Too often, employees aren't given the feedback which helps them know whether they are measuring up to company or management expectations. If no one criticizes their performance, they naturally assume that it's satisfactory and that there's no reason to change. If the employee has not been made aware of the problem before this point, managers should clarify and explain the perceived situation. Once enlightened, the employee may well be willing and able to correct the problem without further ado.

d. THE FRONT-END ANALYSIS

Once you have determined that analyzing the problem is worth the time and effort and that the employee knows about the performance problem, your next step is the front-end analysis. Begin by working through these five questions based on the five steps:

(a) Have we selected the right person for the job? (WHO) If the answer is yes, proceed to (b). If the answer is no, recommend transfer or termination.

(b) Did we provide adequate orientation and direction? (WHAT) If the answer is yes, proceed to (c). If the answer is no, arrange for the appropriate orientation and ongoing direction, then go to (c).

(c) Are there relevant problems in the workplace? (WHERE/WHEN) If the answer is no, proceed to (d). If the answer is yes, correct the problem with the workplace or tools, then go to (d).

(d) Does the employee have the necessary skills? (HOW) If the answer is yes, proceed to (e). If the answer is no, arrange for appropriate training, then go to (e).

(e) Are there deficiencies in the motivational environment? (WHY) If the answer is no, provide coaching (see chapter 8). If the answer is yes, make the necessary changes to increase motivation.

It's important to answer the question at each step before moving on to the next and to proceed with all five steps even when a problem in one area has been identified. In some cases, there may be problems in several areas which need to be identified and remedied. In these cases, you might tackle the lower-ranking problem first, since it is likely to be within your own control as manager. Problems traced to deficiencies in the motivational environment, for example, may be "higher-ranking" ones in the sense that solving them often requires the cooperation of senior management.

If an examination of all five areas fails to identify the source of a performance problem you know exists, you should provide coaching (see chapter 7).

The following case study illustrates the successful application of a front-end analysis conducted according to this method.

Case study

A beverage sales and marketing company employs a number of district managers, each responsible for all the company's brands within a clearly defined geographic area. They ensure that the company's brands are available and visible in retail stores, and they do consumer promotions to increase brand awareness.

Glen Smith has been with the company for ten years, as manager of a district covering the core of a heavily populated city. He has received excellent performance appraisals over the past few years, and he is regularly among the top 10% of district managers in annual bonus earnings.

Glen applies for a district manager position that has come available in a larger but more sparsely populated area. After ten years in the city, he would like a change as well as the challenge of a larger district. He is given the job.

A year after Glen has made the change, he and his manager, Shirley Pletz, get together for a performance appraisal. Both realize that the results are far from satisfactory. Glen is genuinely puzzled. He has worked hard, probably harder than he ever did in his old district. His manager is equally puzzled. One thing Shirley knows for certain, Glen is not a goof-off. Both Glen and Shirley are anxious to identify and correct the problem.

As a people-centered manager who has already had impressive success in analyzing performance problems, Shirley applies the method in a front-end analysis. She has already decided that Glen's problem is worth the time and effort, since revitalizing this valuable ten-year employee is important for the company. Glen is certainly aware of the problem, so it isn't due to lack of feedback.

The first step, determining whether Glen is suitable for the job, takes no time at all. His track record speaks for itself. So Shirley goes immediately to step 2 to see whether Glen has received appropriate job orientation and ongoing direction.

Shirley knows that while Glen was a top performer in his old district, the circumstances and demands of the new one are quite different. Covering a larger district means planning routes more carefully, sequencing calls differently, and calling less frequently than was possible in the old district. Is Glen aware of these and other differences in managing the two districts? Has Shirley given him the direction he needed to adapt to the new situation? As she considers the question, Shirley realizes that she has spent less time with Glen during this last year than she would have spent with a less experienced district manager (she had new people to work with elsewhere). She decides that lack of orientation may well be the problem.

The only way to confirm this diagnosis is to spend time with Glen on the job. If Shirley discovers that Glen has mastered the tricks of running a large district on his own, then she will move on to step 3 in continuing the search for the cause of the problem. If she discovers that her hunch is correct, she knows how to provide the orientation and ongoing direction Glen needs. Furthermore, she will be solving a problem that she herself inadvertently caused, since, as Glen's manager, she is responsible for providing orientation and ongoing direction.

Front-end analysis allows managers to pinpoint problems and solve them. In tracing problems quickly, as Shirley Pletz finds out, managers determine what needs must be addressed before the company enjoys renewed high-quality results.

e. THE TWO LEVELS OF MANAGING

A few years ago, I attended a conference sponsored by Junior Achievement. My curiosity had been piqued by the brochure's description of the target audience for the conference:

- Business leaders who recognize the need to redefine their company's role and values.

- Senior executives who wrestle with the implementation of a powerful vision.

- Top managers who experience dissonance between their values and those of their staff.

- CEOs who are concerned about the bottom line of soft issues, such as Vision and Values.

Clearly, the conference was addressing the issues my management philosophy is all about: building humane organizations with a commitment to developing highly motivated work forces that share the mission of the organization.

111

One of the speakers at the conference, Dr. Lance Secretan, began his presentation by asking the audience, "What do business schools teach?" The audience responded with a predictable list of subjects:

- Managerial finance
- Marketing and marketing communication
- Operations
- Personnel management
- Mergers and acquisitions
- Manufacturing and production
- Business law
- Accounting
- Economics

Dr. Secretan followed this question with a second: "What activities do you consider important that are not taught?" Again, the audience readily responded:

- Leadership
- Turning on the organization
- Translating vision into strategy
- Earning loyalty and enthusiasm
- Implementing change
- Building a team
- Getting grassroots commitment

It was these skills, the "soft" skills of management rather than the "hard" ones taught in business schools, that became the focus for the conference.

Dr. Marti Smye, president of a firm specializing in human relations in organizations undergoing change, used two models (see Sample #6) to illustrate the distinction between what she calls "Hard S" and "Soft S" managing. As Dr.

Smye's models illustrate, "Hard S" managing focuses on the concrete and the tangible: the structure and systems. "Soft S" managing, on the other hand, attends to staffing, leadership style, and skills, all of which flow directly from the organization's shared values and vision. Dr. Smye emphasized that successful organizations depend on a combination of "Hard S" and "Soft S" managing. An ideal model would thus combine the two.

SAMPLE #6
HARD VERSUS SOFT MANAGEMENT STYLES

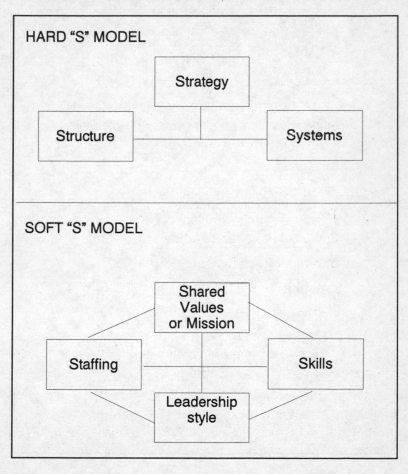

Dr. Stephen R. Covey, an internationally recognized author, lecturer, and teacher has developed a model of "Principle-Centered Leadership" that actually does combine Dr. Smye's two models (see Sample #7).

SAMPLE #7
IDEAL MODEL OF MANAGING

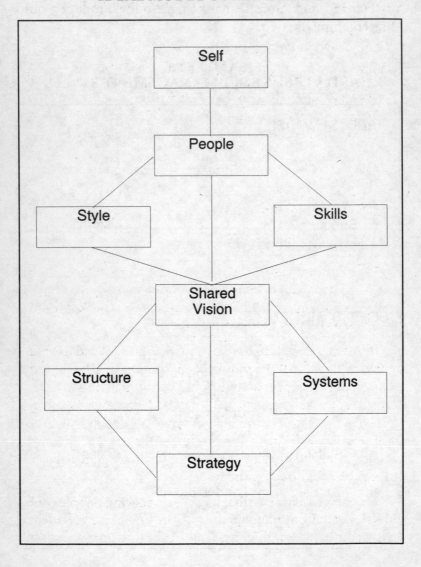

As manager of a department, you don't control the organizational elements of your company, the structure, the systems, or the strategy. However, you are responsible for aligning the work of your department with the company's overall focus. Or, to put it another way, you must translate your company's organizational focus into action in your department. You do this through two steps in managing, namely —

(a) orientation and direction (What), and

(b) workplace and tools (Where and When).

As manager, you do have complete control over the interpersonal part of managing, the "Soft S" part. This aspect includes the other three steps of managing, namely —

(a) staffing or people (Who),

(b) skills (How), and

(c) style or motivation (Why)

f. TAKING THE LEAD

For ideal results, the whole organization, from top to bottom, should be committed to people-centered management. Efficiency, productivity, and a highly motivated work force are the rewards reaped by the organization.

If your organization is not practicing this kind of management, there's all the more reason for you to take the lead in applying the approach in your own department. In any company, the movement toward a better management approach always starts with just one manager. When levels of productivity and motivation rise under his or her leadership, whatever the management level, other managers keen for success rush to discover the reason.

A management style that focuses on solving people problems first can be applied at all times by any manager, at any level of the organization. Every aspect of the manager's task, from selecting people to motivating them, is built into the five steps.

When you use a people-centered management style, you will not only have the right people working for you, who are highly motivated and use their skills and training productively in a work-conducive environment, but you will have highly productive workers as well. So go ahead — be the person responsible for the trend toward higher productivity in your organization. It can all begin with you, the manager.

Taking the lead

g. SUMMARY

In this chapter, we have explored models for understanding the interaction of the five steps of people-centered managing. These models prepare us for a five-point front-end analysis to solve performance problems by first determining their cause.

(a) All five steps or factors, both individually and in combination, influence performance. Effective managers appraise situations by evaluating who does what, where and when, how, and why.

(b) The approach to solving a problem is determined by the cause. Recognizing the cause is already half of the solution.

(c) A front-end analysis will isolate the cause of the problem and predict the solution.

(d) Effective managers organize their analysis according to a flow chart which follows the five steps. Managers and employees share the responsibility for both the problem and the solution.

We then looked at combining the two levels of managing, "Hard S" and "Soft S," for the most productive results.

Finally, we considered the importance of taking the lead in your organization to forge a new, better management style.

Try Worksheet #7 and see whether the management style you currently use allows you to analyze problems in a systematic fashion. Then try Worksheet #8: are you a manager who's willing to take the lead?

WORKSHEET #7
HOW DO YOU ANALYZE A PROBLEM?

Consider your current position and the employees who report to you. Then, ask yourself these questions:

1. Before addressing an apparent problem, do I take time to assess whether the problem is serious enough to warrant my time and attention?

_____

_____

_____

2. Before addressing an apparent problem, do I always check to see whether the employee involved is aware of the problem?

_____

_____

_____

3. In trying to solve a problem, do I always look first for the real cause of the problem?

_____

_____

_____

4. Do I use a disciplined approach, such as a front-end analysis, in determining the cause of a problem?

_____

_____

_____

5. Using the model in Sample #7, can I now find a solution to an employee problem that I have been unable to solve?

_____

_____

_____

These questions may remind you that managing is a skill which must be learned, practiced, and applied according to an organized method rather than a seat-of-the-pants approach.

If you answered no to question 4, you are probably among the majority of managers. Many managers are "too busy" to use a disciplined approach and a thorough analysis to determine the real cause of a problem. However, the old cliché "Haste makes waste" is true in management as it is in other things. Managers must find the real cause of a problem because it is the cause that determines the cure. In other words, without having defined the real problem, applying a cure will be like a stab in the dark or like throwing a dart at a board. We wouldn't think much of the doctor who told us, "I don't know what your problem is, but go on home and to bed and take an aspirin every six hours." We would find it much more acceptable if the doctor said, "I'm not sure what you have, but I'll arrange for some tests and we'll find out." That's what you, as manager, have to do, as well.

WORKSHEET #8
WHAT IS YOUR COMMITMENT TO IMPROVEMENT?

Consider your current position and the employees who report to you. Then, ask yourself these questions:

1. Have I successfully translated the mission and strategy of the company into a focus for action in my department?

_____

_____

_____

_____

_____

2. Do I control appropriately the management steps and principles that fall in my sphere of influence?

_____

_____

_____

_____

_____

3. Do I act on my commitment to the gradual, ongoing improvement of the technology, the workspace, the equipment, the processes, *and* my employees?

_____

_____

_____

_____

_____

4. Is my organization committed to *kaizen* in the sense that it defines the approach to managing people as part of gradual, ongoing improvement everywhere?

_____

_____

_____

_____

_____

5. Am I taking the lead in my organization in applying people-centered managment principles and the *kaizen* concept?

_____

_____

_____

_____

If your organization is not committed to the gradual improvement of all productivity factors including employees, you must take the lead. Other managers will follow.

BIBLIOGRAPHY

Alexander, Christopher. *The Timeless Way of Building.* New York: Oxford University Press, 1979.

De Marco, Tom and Timothy Listen. *Peopleware — Productive Projects and Teams.* New York: Dorset House Publishing Co., 1987.

Fritz, Roger. *Personal Performance Contracts — The Key to Job Success. Los Altos, CA: Crisp Publications, 1987.*

Grensing, Lin. *A Small Business Guide to Employee Selection.* Vancouver, B.C.: Self-Counsel Press, 1991.

If you have enjoyed this book and would like to receive a free catalogue of all Self-Counsel titles, please write to the appropriate address below:

Self-Counsel Press
1481 Charlotte Road
North Vancouver, B.C.
V7J 1H1

Self-Counsel Press
1704 N. State Street
Bellingham, Washington
98225